NEW ZEALAND 2005

Back row left to right: Craig White, Mike Ford, Phil Larder, Dave Reddin, Gareth Jenkins, David McHugh, Andy Robinson, Eddie O'Sullivan, Dave Alred **Fourth row:** Charlie Hodgson, Ronan O'Gara, Matt Stevens, Mark Cueto, Gavin Henson, Gordon D'Arcy, Dwayne Peel, Shane Byrne, Andy Titterrell, Gareth Cooper, Shane Williams **Third row:** Geordan Murphy, Tom Shanklin, Denis Hickie, John Hayes, Gethin Jenkins, Josh Lewsey, Graham Rowntree, Julian White, Ollie Smith, Chris Cusiter **Second row:** Andrew Sheridan, Simon Taylor, Paul O'Connell, Danny Grewcock, Malcolm O'Kelly, Ben Kay, Donncha O'Callaghan, Shane Horgan, Lewis Moody, Steve Thompson, Matt Dawson **Front row:** Will Greenwood, Richard Hill, Jason Robinson, Gordon Bulloch, Martin Corry, Bill Beaumont, Brian O'Driscoll, Sir Clive Woodward, Martyn Williams, Michael Owen, Neil Back, Jonny Wilkinson, Lawrence Dallaglio **Note:** Gareth Thomas and Stephen Jones were not available for the team photo due to playing commitments with their clubs in France

THE TOUGHEST TEST

THE OFFICIAL BOOK OF THE 2005 BRITISH & IRISH LIONS TOUR TO NEW ZEALAND

VSP

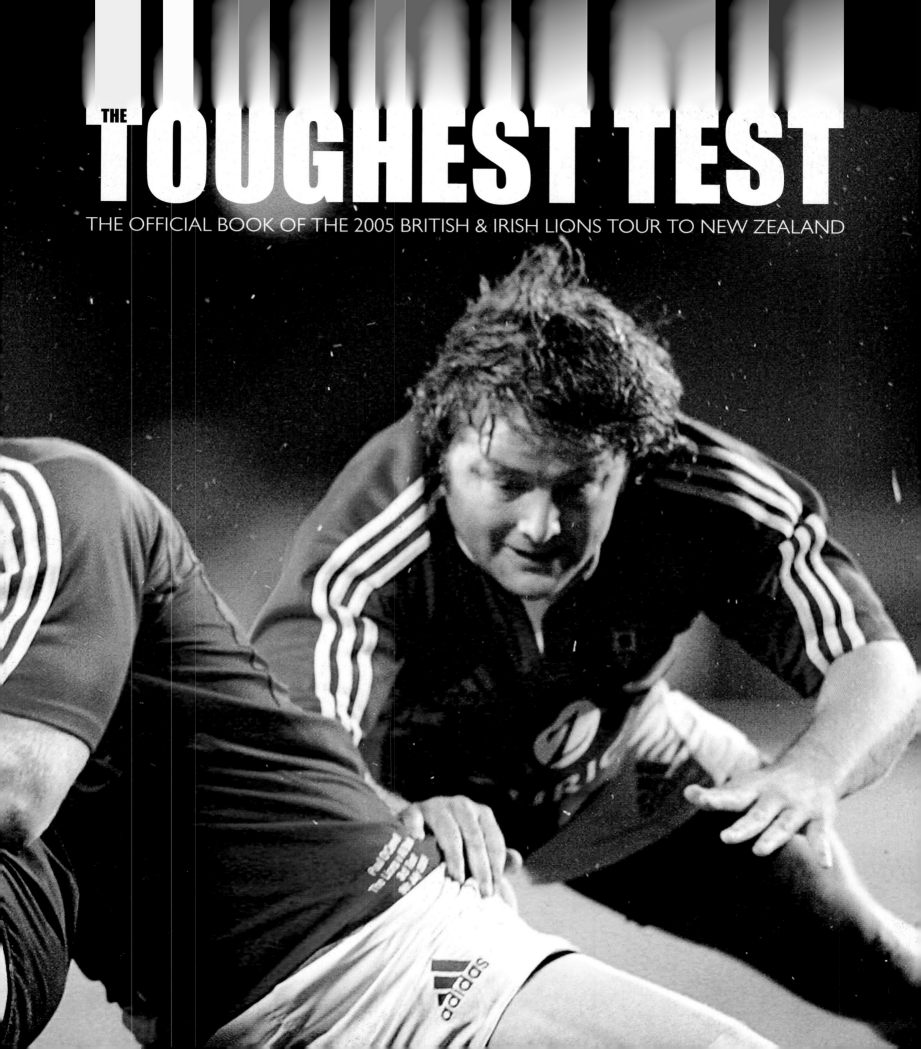

THE TOUGHEST TEST

THE OFFICIAL BOOK OF THE 2005 BRITISH & IRISH LIONS TOUR TO NEW ZEALAND

Contents

FOREWORD by Bill Beaumont 6

INTRODUCTION by Brian O'Driscoll 8

LIONS V ARGENTINA 14

Michael Owen 18

BAY OF PLENTY V LIONS 32

Lawrence Dallaglio 40

TARANAKI V LIONS 46

Chris Cusiter 52

NZ MAORI V LIONS 56

Paul O'Connell 72

WELLINGTON V LIONS 78

Shane Byrne 86

OTAGO V LIONS 90

Ryan Jones 96

SOUTHLAND V LIONS 100

Gavin Henson 104

ALL BLACKS V LIONS 1st Test 108

Martin Corry 120

Neil Back 130

MANAWATU V LIONS 136

Shane Williams 140

ALL BLACKS V LIONS 2nd Test 144

Simon Easterby 166

Gareth Thomas 170

AUCKLAND V LIONS 176

Matt Dawson 184

Gordon Bulloch 188

ALL BLACKS V LIONS 3rd Test 198

Mark Cueto 210

Lewis Moody 218

Stephen Jones 222

JONNY WILKINSON 226

YOU WERE FAN-TASTIC 228

SIR CLIVE WOODWARD 234

LIONS STATS 237

ACKNOWLEDGEMENTS 238

When I came out of the dressing room at the end of the Third Test it confirmed to me that the Lions were not only here to stay, but will go from strength to strength. There were a lot of disappointed players, coaches and medics in that dressing room at Eden Park, but every one of them said they wouldn't change a thing and that they'd had a great rugby experience.

The spirit of the side was magnificent and I, for one, am proud to have been associated with the Lions of 2005. And that pride is one of the reasons why I feel honoured to write this Foreword for the official book of the tour. It's a fabulous account of our trip to New Zealand with the personal – and exclusive – accounts of the players and some sensational photographs from Getty Images.

The one group of people I must thank is the Lions supporters. This book is for you. I don't think there has ever been such a migration of rugby supporters across the world in the history of our game. The New Zealand Department of Labour estimates that around 29,000 people made the trip, but with the noise they made and the colour they brought to the streets it sometimes felt like there were 290,000 of them.

Everywhere we went the fans supported and cheered us. Even when we arrived back in Auckland towards the end of the tour, after we had gone 2-0 down in the series, there they were clapping us into our hotel. I hope those fans

appreciate how grateful we were f or their support and, like the rest of the squad, all I wish is that we could have delivered a victory for them.

Lions tours have always had Welsh, English, Irish and Scottish standing together in a brotherhood of rugby, but this time the spirit was taken to an even higher plane. I remember after we lost the First Test in Christchurch, Clive asked the players and management not to hide in their hotels but to go out into the streets and meet the fans. Their magnificent support meant an awful lot to every member of the Lions squad, both players and management.

Unfortunately we couldn't give those fantastic supporters the victory we all craved, but I would like to take this opportunity to congratulate the All Blacks on the way they played to win the series. They were magnificent.

New Zealand is an incredibly difficult place to come and play. You only have to experience what rugby means to the people of New Zealand to realise that; it is no wonder that only one Lions team in the side's great history has won in this country. Those legendary players of 1971 were a unique team and it is to the regret of every single member of the 2005 party that we couldn't emulate the deeds of players like Gareth Edwards, Barry John and Mervyn Davies. The Lions have gone to New Zealand eleven times and lost on ten of those

occasions, so that gives you an idea of the size of the task we had in front of us.

But that's not to say that every member of the Lions 2005 squad didn't give everything they had on those fields of Jade Stadium, Westpac Stadium and Eden Park. They gave all they had, but it wasn't enough. In hindsight, we were probably two or three games short of what a real Lions tour should be, and has been in the past. Certainly most of the coaches would have liked a few extra games.

But the players we took from Britain and Ireland were desperate to play rugby for the Lions. They wanted to play Test rugby and, above all, they wanted to be playing in winning sides for the Lions. So, although there is huge disappointment, I can't think of any player who would say to me that he didn't enjoy the experience or that he wouldn't want to play for the Lions in South Africa in 2009. And don't forget the achievement of Ian McGeechan's midweek side, who won all five of their bruising matches – no mean feat in a rugby-mad country like New Zealand.

Looking back there really isn't anything I would change. We definitely picked the right number of players to go to New Zealand, especially if you consider the number of injuries we picked up. The party was not too big and the hardest-working people on the tour were the medical staff and the physios, who did a tremendous job.

Much has also been said about the cost of bringing so many players and coaches around the world, but this tour is the first that has made a profit and we should be proud of that.

The players have told me that, despite losing the Test Series, they've learnt a hell of a lot from the trip. They have been fantastic ambassadors for their countries and for the Lions and that is crucial. Yes, the most important thing to us was winning the Test Series, but almost equally important was that the Lions ethos continues.

We enjoyed being in New Zealand and I know New Zealand enjoyed having us and our supporters in their country. You only had to be on the tour to see what the Lions mean to the rugby community. Wherever we went the welcome was overwhelming and I hope your reaction to this official account of the tour is as good. This book gives you a unique insight into a Lions tour – a one-off in sport and an institution that is going from strength to strength.

See you in South Africa in four years' time!

My Lions captaincy may have only lasted just over 40 seconds, but I still look back on the trip to New Zealand with pride and affection.

Of course sides are judged on their Test results, but I can take many positives from this tour and flicking through this official book brings the memories flooding back.

I can hardly describe how proud I was leading out the Lions for the First Test in Christchurch. But to leave on a stretcher – just like Lawrence Dallaglio had against the Bay of Plenty – was definitely not in the plan.

I still value my place, and the place of the 2005 side, in Lions history. I may only have captained the Test side for a short time but I take pride in the fact that I am part of a small band of rugby players, and an even smaller band of Irishmen, to lead this great team. When I was asked to be captain I regarded it as a rare honour and I still do now – although I would have preferred to have done the job for a little longer!

Trips like this is are one-offs. The Lions of 2005 will never play together again, so you have to enjoy it as much as you can on and off the pitch. Losing 3-0 hurt – and that is how we'll be judged – but it doesn't take the shine off the Lions and it doesn't change the fact that this is a very special team with unique values. I sincerely hope the Lions go on for many years to come and there's no reason why they shouldn't.

There were a lot of new friendships made out in New Zealand and the guys who hadn't been on Lions tours before now realise how special a team it is. There were players on this trip that I had only played against, only seen at after-match dinners, but now I would count them as my friends. That aspect gives you a taste for more. Once you have played for the Lions all you want to do is have that feeling again.

My well-publicised exit from the tour is now firmly behind me and I'm looking forward to my return to the field. I was obviously angry at the time, but I have now managed to put it behind me. You can't dwell on these things or they will drive you crazy.

Subsequently, Tana [Umaga] and Keven [Mealamu] came up to me to explain that there had been no malice in their tackle and you have to take their apologies at face value. You have to take them at their word. Of course I was upset that no sanctions were taken after the match, but there comes a time when you have to move on. I've also been the culprit of some bad tackles in my time and I think once you accept responsibility you have just got to get on with it.

Off the pitch I don't think my relationship or my friendship with Tana will be changed in any shape or form. I will still go and have a drink with him after a game. We will carry on as we did before. I still respect him hugely as a rugby player and I think what happens on the pitch is separate to what happens off it.

We must acknowledge how well the All Blacks played. It is the best I have seen them play in a long time. I think that when you play against them you have to try and chip away leads against them and try to take their confidence away. If you don't, they get into that inspired form and there is no stopping them. They start to feed on confidence and the passes begin to stick.

We didn't play badly against them - it's just that they played extremely well. Occasionally you come up against teams like that and you have to hold your hand up.

I'm sure that if we did this tour again there would be things we'd do slightly differently. But one thing that everyone knows now, if they didn't already, is that the game has moved on in an incredible way. I'm sure everyone appreciates we would have done better if the side had been together longer, but that's the whole challenge – it's what the Lions is all about.

One thing that worked particularly well, and should now be set in stone, is the two coaching groups: one for midweek games and one for Saturday matches. With so many players on board, there is really no choice. I disagree with those people who have criticised the number of players we took. We ended up leaving Heathrow with 45 players, but there is an argument for saying we needed 55, considering the intensity of international rugby today and the players we lost through the tour. Let's not forget, we didn't just have three Tests to play but eight other games also, and it is likely that will be the same in 2009. It is hard to play Wednesday-Saturday, but with fewer players you might be asking guys to play Wednesday-Saturday-Wednesday. The game is far more physical now than it has been on previous Lions tours.

I don't think you can fully appreciate the unique nature of the Lions until you take part in a tour and, for me, that realisation came in 2001 when I went to Australia. Despite the way things turned out, I am honoured to have experienced it again.

I sincerely hope that you enjoy this fantastic book... and here's to 2009 and beyond!

"I have a dream"

Sir Clive unveils his coaching team, the iconic 2005 Lions jersey by adidas, and checks out Jade Stadium on a pre-tour fact-finding mission

April 11th 2005: The Lions head coach unveils his initial 44 man squad and announces that Brian O'Driscoll will become Ireland's first Lions captain since 1983

The long road ahead: No summer holidays just yet for the 45 players selected for the 2005 Lions as they knuckle down for the arrival of Argentina in Cardiff

John Hayes, Ronan O'Gara, Ben Kay and Michael Owen are presented with their match shirts, on the morning of the Argentina game, by Lions legends Bill Beaumont and Ian McGeechan

Cardiff

Cardiff is a city steeped in rugby tradition. Located where the famous Arms Park used to stand the 74,000 capacity Millennium Stadium – with its' closing roof and dynamic views from all seats – has further enhanced the city's sporting credentials.

Cardiff Wales

The Zurich Test
The Lions v Argentina
23rd May 2005

ZURICH

MILLENNIUM STADIUM, CARDIFF
Kick Off 7.45pm   Gates Open 6.00pm
GATE 1   STAIR 12 LEVEL 6 AISLE 634
BLOCK U34   ROW 3   SEAT 11
TICKETMASTER

002
TO BE RETAINED

£56.00

ENTER BY GATE COLOUR (SEE OVER)

Win a limited edition signed jersey!

turn over for details

LIONS
v ARGENTINA
23rd MAY 2005

With the squad selected, the captain revealed and the 2005 strip unveiled – and selling faster than any replica shirt in history – the Lions gathered at the Vale of Glamorgan Hotel in Wales.

Sir Clive Woodward had lined up Argentina as pre-tour opponents at the Millennium Stadium in what would be only the third-ever Lions match on home soil. With local hero Michael Owen selected to captain the team, fresh from lifting the Six Nations trophy on this very turf, and Jonny Wilkinson named in the starting line-up, the city of Cardiff was buzzing with anticipation. But this was to be no exhibition match. Woodward knew the rapidly-improving Pumas would provide a stern test for his New Zealand-bound men... and so it proved.

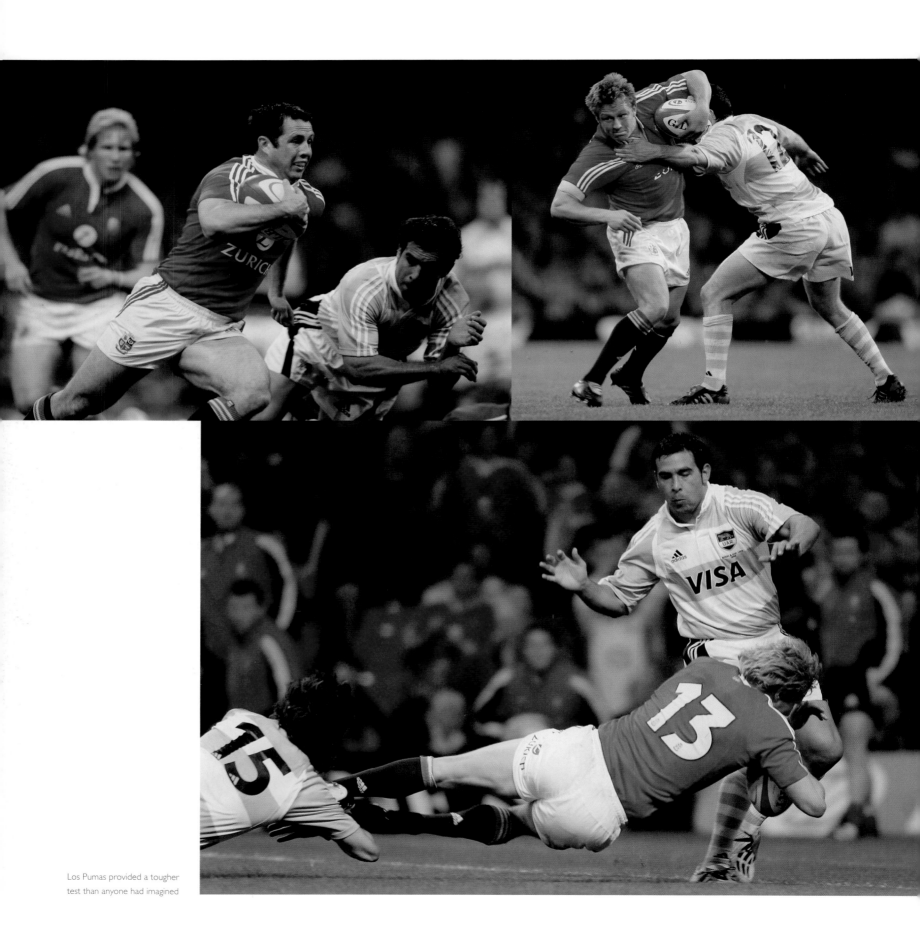

Los Pumas provided a tougher
test than anyone had imagined

Becoming part of the British & Irish Lions team was everything I had dreamt of. Magnificent. Things had been a bit of a whirl since March, when Wales clinched the Grand Slam, so to meet up with the rest of the Lions at the end of April ensured another chapter in this unbelievable season for me.

I know it is a cliché, but the truth is that I grew up in south Wales pretending to be a Lion. School and club games of rugby had me imagining being Mervyn Davies or John Taylor galloping down the touchline. So to become a Lion, just like they were back in the 1970s, is the realisation of that dream.

You dream about it, but you never really know what it is like until you meet your fellow Lions for the first time and see the quality of players in the room. That brings it home. Then when you think of the people who haven't been picked, you realise how lucky you are, how privileged you are to be in that room.

Ian McGeechan and Bill Beaumont presented us with our jerseys before the Argentina game and all I could think of was that it was like being in that *Living with the Lions* video, which was shot on the 1997 tour to South Africa, and which I have watched over and over again. It was emotional and hard getting it ;all to sink in.

By then we'd already been together for two weeks and even before that we'd been receiving regular letters, cards and even Lions wristbands from Clive Woodward.

Obviously I knew of every one of the other 44 players in the squad but, apart from the Welsh boys, I didn't really know them. People might say the English are arrogant, but come on a Lions tour and you'll discover that is rubbish. You have a perception of people and then you meet them and train with them and it changes. Everyone was brilliant. And with such quality players around there are fewer dropped balls than ever before and fewer mistakes. It makes you raise your game even in training.

Then when I was told I would captain the Lions in front of my home crowd in Cardiff – well, to be honest, I'm still pinching myself to make sure that wasn't a dream. The only downside was that we didn't put in the performance we wanted to against Argentina and we were disappointed with a draw. Maybe people were a little too anxious to impress, but I also think people under-estimate Argentine rugby. They played fantastically well. For us it was all about preparing for the tour and we knew we still had six games before the First Test to get it right.

It's all about handling the pressure – a bit like giving a speech at the Lions' Farewell dinner at Cardiff Arms Park after the match. I don't mind making those speeches, it's all part of being the captain, but I was a little stumped when the Argentineans brought up a guy from Patagonia who spoke perfect Welsh. Unfortunately I don't speak a word, but luckily David Pickering from the WRU came to my rescue.

After negotiating that tricky hurdle it felt like taking on the All Blacks would be a breeze!

He's back: The left boot of returning hero
Jonny Wilkinson seals a 25-25 draw with
an injury time kick, but it was the Pumas
celebrating at the final whistle (*right*)

WRU

LIONS   25
PUMAS   25

THE
LIONS
FOUR NATIONS ONE TEAM

LIONS 25		ARGENTINA 25
Geordan Murphy	15	Bernardo Stortoni
Denis Hickie	14	Núñez Piossek
Ollie Smith (Shane Horgan, 60 mins)	13	Lisandro Arbizu
Gordon D'Arcy	12	Felipe Contepomi (Captain)
Shane Williams	11	Francisco Leonelli
Jonny Wilkinson (Vice Captain)	10	Federico Todeschini (Francisco Bosch, 72 mins)
Gareth Cooper (Chris Cusiter, 60 mins)	9	Nicolás Fernández Miranda
Graham Rowntree	1	Federico Méndez
Shane Byrne (Steve Thompson, 71 mins)	2	Mario Ledesma
John Hayes (Julian White, 55 mins)	3	Mauricio Reggiardo
Donncha O'Callaghan	4	Pablo Bouza (Manuel Carizza, 68 mins)
Danny Grewcock (Ben Kay, 71 mins)	5	Mariano Sambucetti
Martin Corry	6	Federico Genoud
Lewis Moody	7	Martín Schusterman (Santiago Sanz, 61 mins)
Michael Owen (Captain)	8	Juan Manuel Leguizamón

Replacements (unused): Ronan O'Gara, Lawrence Dallaglio

Replacements (unused): Eusebio Guinazu, Leopoldo De Chazal, Lucio Lopez, Federico Serra

Try: Smith

Try: Piossek

Con: Wilkinson

Con: Todeschini

Pens: Wilkinson 6

Pens: Todeschini 6

REFEREE: Stuart Dickinson (Australia)

NEW ZEALAND 2005

Pride of place

The Journey Begins...

Now boarding squad numbers
1-20: The Lions take up a departure
lounge of their own as they depart
from Heathrow

The Lions arrive at Auckland airport and receive a heroes' welcome from their travelling supporters....

... and an impromptu haka from
local All Blacks fan, Pohatu Albert
(*far right*), as New Zealand gears up
to repel the Lions 'invasion'

Lion trainers: Malcolm O'Kelly and Simon Taylor *(right)* put in the hard graft, little knowing their tours will be cruelly short-lived, while *(below)* front row forwards Andy Sheridan and Steve Thompson get busy with the weights...

... and backs Josh Lewsey, Brian O'Driscoll and Mark Cueto show off their silky skills with the round ball

Bay of Plenty

Named Bay of Plenty by
Captain Cook in the 18th
Century when he sailed in to
the area aboard Endeavour,
the Bay of Plenty in New
Zealand's stunningly
bountiful Rotorua area
is one of New Zealand's
premier tourist destinations.

DURING THE BLACKOUT

FOLLOW THE DRILL:

1. KEEP VIGIL BY YOUR TELEPHONE
2. GO TO UNITEFORVICTORY.CO.NZ FOR THE LATEST INTELLIGENCE
3. AMASS YOUR FORCES WITH PUSH 2 TALK
4. DO NOT ENGAGE THE ROTUND-SUNBURNT-KNOTTED-HANKIE-WEARING ENEMY

THE LIONS ARE INVADING
UNITE FOR VICTORY!

Telecom
WHEN THE INVADER COMES
YOU NEED TO BE READY
WWW.UNITEFORVICTORY.CO.NZ

BAY OF PLENTY v LIONS

4th JUNE 2005

Barely a week after touching down at Auckland airport, and with the excitement and anticipation reaching fever pitch both in New Zealand and back home (where the Lions jersey was undoubtedly becoming the fashion item of the summer), Sir Clive Woodward named a strong side for the first match of the tour against Bay of Plenty in the stunning Rotorua region. Skipper O'Driscoll, veteran Lawrence Dallaglio and Welsh stars Peel, Henson and Shane & Martyn Williams were all included against the Steamers – formed in 1911 and the inaugural winners of the NPC – whose rich rugby pedigree includes a victory over Fiji in 1970. "No-one is under any illusions as to the challenge we face," said Dallaglio on the eve of the match.

The big kick off: With the 11th Lions
tour of New Zealand about to explode
into action, everyone has dressed up for
the occasion

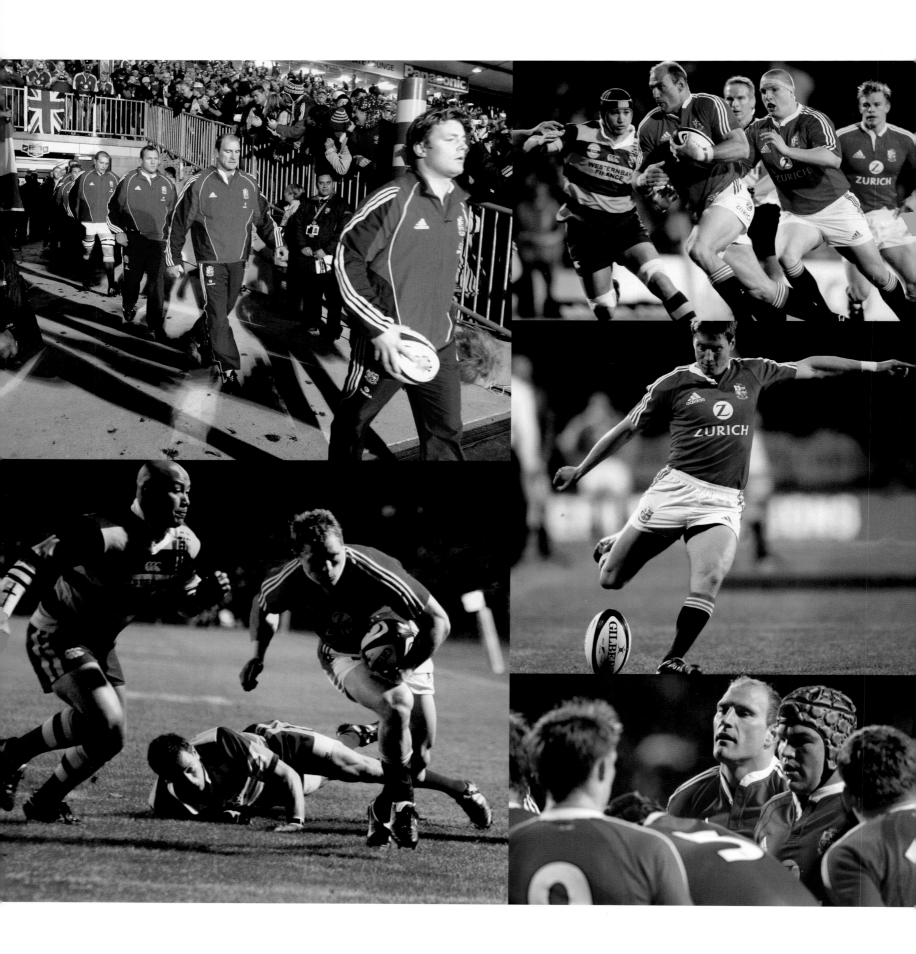

Points-a-Plenty: After a superb first
15 minutes of error-free rugby the
Lions tragically lose Dallaglio, but
still rack up 34 points and a first
hard-fought victory of the tour

Peel power: Dwayne makes an early
bid for the number 9 Test jersey
with a solid scrum-half performance

I knew the moment I hit the ground that my Lions tour was over. I approached Brian O'Driscoll to help him make a tackle but the guy cut inside, so I speeded up to grab him. The pitches out in New Zealand can be really dewy and just before I made the tackle I slipped. My studs got caught in the ground but my body kept on going so, as I went over, I felt my ankle rotate and then go forward. Then when I hit the ground I could feel my foot was pointing in the wrong direction

As I lay on the ground I was in a lot of pain, as the ankle was both fractured and dislocated, with the dislocation being the more painful injury of the two. But fortunately as soon as the Lions doctor, James Robson, and physio, Bob Stewart, got on the pitch James was able to put the dislocation back in. As soon as he did that the pain receded. James said he'd never put a dislocated ankle back in on a pitch before. He did a great job and then the recovery started.

Of course at the time I wasn't thinking about the long-term or even the fact that I was going to miss the tour. You don't worry too much about things like that straight away. You're more concerned about reducing the pain and getting the injury sorted.

Ringing home later brought me back down to earth a little as my daughter, Ella, came on the phone to say: "We were worried about you daddy, I've never seen you taken off on a stretcher before... but you did look funny going off the pitch on a golf cart!". That certainly made me smile.

The most frustrating thing, of course, was that I really felt on top of my game going into the match. On the back of beating Leicester in the Premiership Final, I was starting to get into my best form. I was in good shape and for the first 15 minutes of the match I felt great and we were playing well as a team.

We had come out of the changing room steaming. If anyone was 'The Steamers' it was us and not them. After scoring three tries in ten minutes I felt we were really going to go on and ram home the message that the Lions had arrived.

They did score a try before I went off, but I think the whole incident – not just because it was me – gave Bay of Plenty a chance to re-gather themselves. They were able to recover and make it a far closer scoreline than it would have been.

A lot of people drew comparisons between this injury and the Lions tour of 2001, when I was forced home from Australia with a knee problem. But perhaps what they forget is that I have been lucky enough to play in a winning Lions Series in South Africa in 1997. From my point of view that brings me some comfort. I have worn the Lions Test jersey and enjoyed a Series victory.

I've done it once, but I so badly wanted to do it again.

Rotorua International Stadium
ATTENDANCE: 33,000

BAY OF PLENTY 20		LIONS 34
Adrian Cashmore	15	Josh Lewsey
Filimoni Bolovucu (Apoua Stewart, 50 mins)	14	Mark Cueto
Allan Bunting	13	Brian O'Driscoll (Captain)
Grant McQuoid	12	Gavin Henson (Gordon D'Arcy, 69 mins)
Anthony Tahana	11	Tom Shanklin (Matt Dawson, 77 mins)
Murray Williams	10	Ronan O'Gara
Kevin Senio	9	Dwayne Peel
Simms Davison (Taufa'ao Filise, 63 mins)	1	Gethin Jenkins
Aleki Lutui	2	Gordon Bulloch (Steve Thompson, 65 mins)
Ben Castle	3	Matt Stevens (Andy Sheridan, 65 mins)
Mark Sorenson (Paul Tupai, 63 mins)	4	Paul O'Connell
Bernie Upton	5	Ben Kay
Wayne Ormond (Captain)	6	Richard Hill
Nili Latu	7	Martyn Wiliams
Colin Bourke (Warren Smith, 45 mins)	8	Lawrence Dallaglio (Vice Captain) (Martin Corry, 21 mins)

Replacements (unused): Donncha O'Callaghan, Charlie Hodgson

Tries: Bourke, Williams

Con: Williams 2

Pens: Williams 2

Tries: Lewsey 2, Cueto, Shanklin, Peel, D'Arcy

Con: O'Gara 2

REFEREE: Paul Honiss (New Zealand)

Cloud nine: Boosted by a win in game one, the Lions prepare for Taranaki at their scenic Takapuna training camp near Auckland

New Plymouth, Taranaki

Set in the shadow of the beautiful, snow-capped Mount Taranaki, it is possible to ski and surf on the same afternoon in the Taranaki region . The drive from the mountain plateau to the beach takes just half an hour.

MATCH **2**

Taranaki
versus
British & Irish Lions

Wednesday June 8, 2005 at 7.10 pm, Yarrow Stadium, New Plymouth

$7.00

OFFICIAL

LIONS SERIES 2005

PROGRAMME

TARANAKI
R T F
RUGBY

NEW ZEALAND 2005

TARANAKI v LIONS
8th JUNE 2005

After the hard-fought win over Bay of Plenty, no-one in the Lions camp was expecting things to get any easier against Taranaki in New Plymouth. One of the strongest of the provincial New Zealand teams, Taranaki have a rich history against the visitors – indeed they were the first side in the world ever to defeat the Lions, beating the 1888 tourists 1-0 (in the days of one point for a try). And, as if to emphasise what playing against the Lions means here, on the eve of the match 22 year-old Samoan wing Sailosi Tagicakibau remarkably declared himself fit to play.

"It's a once in a lifetime opportunity," he said, "and I wasn't going to miss it because of a broken bone in my leg."

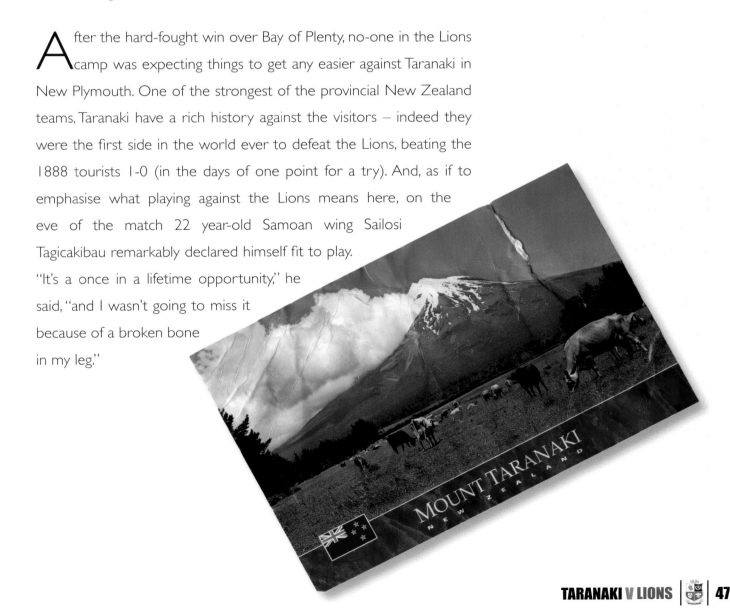

(Previous page) Tries for Corry, Horgan and Murphy (2) give the Lions fans in New Plymouth plenty to cheer about

Andy Titterrell *(above right)* leads the way, Danny Grewcock *(right)* takes charge and Graham Rowntree *(far right)* makes some new friends!

Pulling on the Lions shirt against Taranaki was the biggest achievement of my life so far. There is so much history around the Lions jersey, and so many great players have worn it, that I felt a huge weight of responsibility on my shoulders. I regard playing for the Lions as a great honour and a fantastic opportunity to be part of something incredibly special.

The first half was tough, and we were coming off second best in a number of areas, but after half-time I really started to enjoy myself. We were playing well and scoring tries and that's always a great feeling.

The forwards made it easy for us in the second half. Martin Corry got the boys going and if you have that sort of go-forward ball you can start to play good rugby.

A Lions tour is all about new partnerships, playing with guys you've only seen in the opposition ranks before, and I really enjoyed working with Charlie Hodgson. Charlie controlled it brilliantly. He kicked superbly and his passing was outstanding. He is a very easy No 10 to play inside, so I hope people felt we linked up well. If I got another chance to play with him, I'd be pretty excited about it.

Success for me on the trip would have been a Test Series victory for the Lions first, with me playing in the Tests second. I realise I am young and not the front-runner at the moment but, believe me, I didn't go on the tour to make up the numbers or back up anyone else.

I want to be the Test scrum-half in the future and I'll do all I can to achieve that ambition.

Chris Cusiter

ATTENDANCE: 22,000

TARANAKI 14		**LIONS 36**
Scott Ireland (Brendon Watt, 15 mins)	15	Geordan Murphy
Sailosi Tagicakibau (Matt Harvey, 40 mins)	14	Shane Horgan
Mark Stewart	13	Will Greenwood (Vice Captain)
Lifeimi Mafi	12	Ollie Smith
Chris Woods	11	Denis Hickie
Sam Young	10	Charlie Hodgson
Craig Fevre (James King, 63 mins)	9	Chris Cusiter (Gareth Cooper, 51 mins)
Tony Penn (Hamish Mitchell, 69 mins)	1	Graham Rowntree
Andrew Hore (Phil Mitchell, 75 mins)	2	Andy Titterrell (Shane Byrne, 66 mins)
Gordon Slater	3	John Hayes (Gethin Jenkins, 48 mins)
Paul Tito (Captain)	4	Donncha O'Callaghan
Scott Breman (Jason Eaton, 64 mins)	5	Danny Grewcock
John Willis	6	Martin Corry (Captain)
Chris Masoe	7	Lewis Moody
Tomasi Soqeta (Richard Bryant, 63 mins)	8	Michael Owen

Replacements (unused): Ben Kay, Martyn Williams, Jonny Wilkinson, Gavin Henson

Tries: Mascoe, Watt

Tries: Horgan, Murphy 2

Cons: Young 2

Cons: Hodgson 2

Sin-bin: Andrew Hore (54mins)

Pens: Hodgson 4

REFEREE: Kelvin Deaker (New Zealand)

NEW ZEALAND 2005

The British & Irish Lions would like to thank

Official Sponsor

Official Kit Supplier

Official Partners

GUINNESS

Official Suppliers

Hamilton

Hamilton is New Zealand's fourth largest city and 11 per cent of the region's population are of Maori descent. Indeed, the area was the scene of a fierce war between British troops and the Waikito Maori in the mid 1800s, after which more than 450,000 hectares of land was taken from the Maori and given to British soldiers. No wonder they were out for revenge!

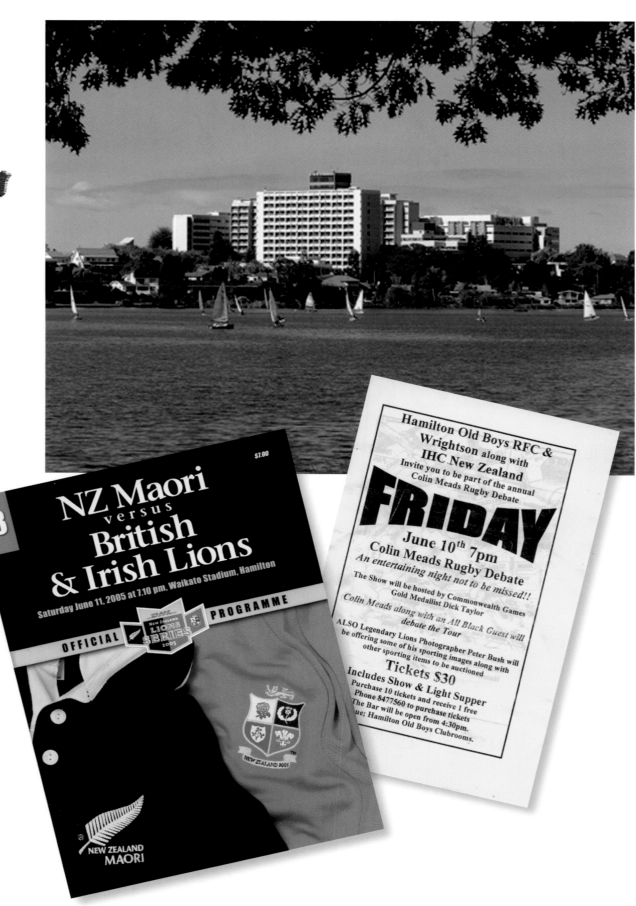

$7.00

MATCH 3

NZ Maori
versus
British
& Irish Lions

Saturday June 11, 2005 at 7.10 pm, Waikato Stadium, Hamilton

OFFICIAL PROGRAMME

NEW ZEALAND
LIONS SERIES 2005

NEW ZEALAND 2005

NEW ZEALAND
MAORI

Hamilton Old Boys RFC & Wrightson along with IHC New Zealand
Invite you to be part of the annual Colin Meads Rugby Debate

FRIDAY
June 10th 7pm
Colin Meads Rugby Debate
An entertaining night not to be missed!!

The Show will be hosted by Commonwealth Games Gold Medallist Dick Taylor

Colin Meads along with an All Black Guest will debate the Tour

ALSO Legendary Lions Photographer Peter Bush will be offering some of his sporting images along with other sporting items to be auctioned

Tickets $30
Includes Show & Light Supper

Purchase 10 tickets and receive 1 free
Phone 8477560 to purchase tickets
The Bar will be open from 4:30pm.
...ue; Hamilton Old Boys Clubrooms.

NZ MAORI
v LIONS
11th JUNE 2005

Two down and nine to go, but the Lions' next challenge would be as tough as they come. Considered the strongest non-Test playing team in the world, the New Zealand Maori – made up of players with at least one 16th Maori descent – had only ever lost four of their 26 matches. And although they had never beaten the Lions (despite being 20-0 up at half-time in 1993), they had beaten England and Argentina. And with no fewer than nine past or present All Blacks in his starting line-up – plus the legendary Carlos Spencer on the bench – coach Matt Te Pou had named one of the strongest Maori teams ever. It was exactly the pre-Test challenge that Woodward wanted and to face it he went for power by selecting the heaviest front row in Lions history – Andrew Sheridan, Steve Thompson and Julian White, weighing in at a collective 348kg.

Country roads: Matt Stevens provides the soundtrack for the coach journey to Hamilton, while Donncha O'Callaghan grabs an uncomfortable-looking forty winks

With the dressing room all kitted out, physio Bob Stewart (*left*) checks the programme to see if he got a mention, while his colleagues Phil Pask and Stuart Barton share a pre-match joke.

(*Above*) Team doctor Gary O'Driscoll and Bob Stewart compare last-minute notes

The Maori lay down their challenge to the Lions with their very own haka. Derived from the Maori words Ha (breathe) and Ka (to ignite), Ha-Ka literally means "to ignite the breath"

Playing with fierce passion and power, the Maori live up to their potential, while the Lions struggle to find their best form

Leon MacDonald scrambles the ball over the line for a crucial first-half score

The second-half arrival of Carlos Spencer (*right*) for his farewell appearance galvanizes the Maori to new heights and, despite a late rally and O'Driscoll score, the Lions go down 19-13

NZ MAORI 19
THE LIONS 13
37 19

Martyn Williams suffers in
silence, as the Maori players
celebrate a famous victory

The Lions picked the perfect person to present us with our jerseys before the Maori match, but unfortunately we couldn't do Lawrence Dallaglio justice on the pitch.

We all felt for Lawrence when we saw him break his ankle against Bay of Plenty and it was a stroke of genius by Clive Woodward to bring him back into the squad for this game.

Before he gave us our jerseys Lawrence talked well about the friends and family we had back home. He reminded us about all they had done for us over the years and said that when we ran out on the pitch we would be playing for them.

I have played against Lawrence many times, but having him on the same side makes you realise what an inspirational figure he is. Unfortunately, we failed to live up to his fine words and that made it all the more disappointing to lose in a Lions jersey. It hurt.

It was an incredibly tough game, played at Test standard, but the most disappointing thing was that we didn't match them for competitive aggression. They were more aggressive than us at the breakdown; they were more aggressive than us all over the pitch and that was a big lesson for us - a big wake up call.

You know you will have bad days in rugby, but the mark of a good side is how you react to them. When you lose a big game, the following week normally sees a very good performance. That is the way it is with Ireland and the way it is with Munster, and that was how we were determined it would be with the Lions.

After the game the whole 45 man Lions squad crowded into our tiny changing room in Hamilton. It was symbolic of the way we all stood together on the tour.

Then the next day we went jet-boating and just tried to relax. To come out to New Zealand and do stuff like that was great. Everyone was getting on well and the 'craic' was brilliant throughout the squad. The banter was flying around and that is what touring is all about. It took our minds off the rugby and that kind of thing really freshens you up for the next day's training.

By the time we got back to work, we felt that the good thing about the Maori game was that we wouldn't arrive at the Tests with the problems we had at the breakdown and the problems we had at the line-out. We planned to sort those things out.

When you look at the boys in Australia in 2001, they lost a game midway through. In 1997 they also lost a game before the First Test. So we started to look at the defeat as a way of helping us to nail down a few problems – a big thing for us if we were to follow in the footsteps of the past two Lions Series and win the First Test.

NZ MAORI 19   LIONS 13

NZ MAORI		LIONS
Leon MacDonald	15	Josh Lewsey
Rico Gear	14	Tom Shanklin
Rua Tipoki	13	Brian O'Driscoll (Captain)
Luke McAlister	12	Gordon D'Arcy (Shane Horgan, 22-29 mins)
Caleb Ralph	11	Shane Williams
David Hill (Carlos Spencer, 42 mins)	10	Stephen Jones (Ronan O'Gara, 30-36 mins)
Piri Weepu	9	Matt Dawson
Deacon Manu (Greg Feek, 52 mins)	1	Andy Sheridan (Gethin Jenkins, 49 mins)
Corey Flynn	2	Steve Thompson (Shane Byrne, 72 mins)
Carl Hayman	3	Julian White
Ross Filipo (Daniel Braid, 72 mins)	4	Simon Shaw
Sean Hohneck	5	Paul O'Connell (Vice Captain)
Jono Gibbes (Captain)	6	Richard Hill
Marty Holah	7	Martyn Williams
Angus MacDonald	8	Michael Owen (Gethin Jenkins, 42-49 mins)

Replacements (unused): Scott Linklater, Wayne Ormond, Craig McGrath, Neil Brew

Replacements (unused): Ben Kay, Simon Easterby, Dwayne Peel

Try: L MacDonald

Try: O'Driscoll

Con: McAlister

Con: Jones

Pens: Hill 2, McAlister 2

Pens: Jones 2

Sin-bin: Sheridan (39 mins)

REFEREE: Steve Walsh (New Zealand)

As if to prove there is no corner of New Zealand untouched by a passion for rugby, pupils of Christ's College in Christchurch perform the haka for the visiting Lions

Wellington

Situated between a beautiful harbour and the rolling green North Island hills, Wellington is the capital city of New Zealand and the gateway to a wealth of natural beauty.

TRANSLATIONS FOR LIONS SUPPORTERS

HEINZ = WATTIES
TETLEY'S TEA = BELL TEA
MARMITE = VEGEMITE
FOOTBALL = RUGBY
BRITISH ALE = BAR BODEGA

For a proper English breakfast & the only place in Wellington fo hand pulled Ales…

BAR BODE

101 Ghuznee St

MATCH 4

Wellington
versus
British
& Irish Lions

Wednesday June 15, 2005 at 7.10 pm, Westpac Stadium, Wellington

OFFICIAL LIONS SERIES 2005 PROGRAMME

$7.00

WELLINGTON LIONS

WELLINGTON v LIONS
15th JUNE 2005

Out of the frying pan and into the fire. After the shattering disappointment of defeat by the Maori, the Lions of Britain & Ireland travelled to New Zealand's capital city to take on the Lions of Wellington. Even without Test stars Tana Umaga, Conrad Smith, Rodney So'oialo and Jerry Collins, the reigning New Zealand champions would provide yet another huge challenge.

Sir Clive Woodward, meanwhile, reacted to the Maori defeat by stepping up the intensity of the Lions' training sessions and naming a Test-strength side for the Wellington clash, with first tour appearances for World Cup winners Jonny Wilkinson, Jason Robinson and Neil Back, in addition to Wales skipper Gareth Thomas. "Coming to this country was never going to be easy, the history books show that," said Woodward. "It will be a big side out on Wednesday and we've got to accept the disappointment, learn the right lessons and move on very strongly."

Jason Robinson, at his unstoppable
best, blasting past Wellington's
Ma'a Nonu

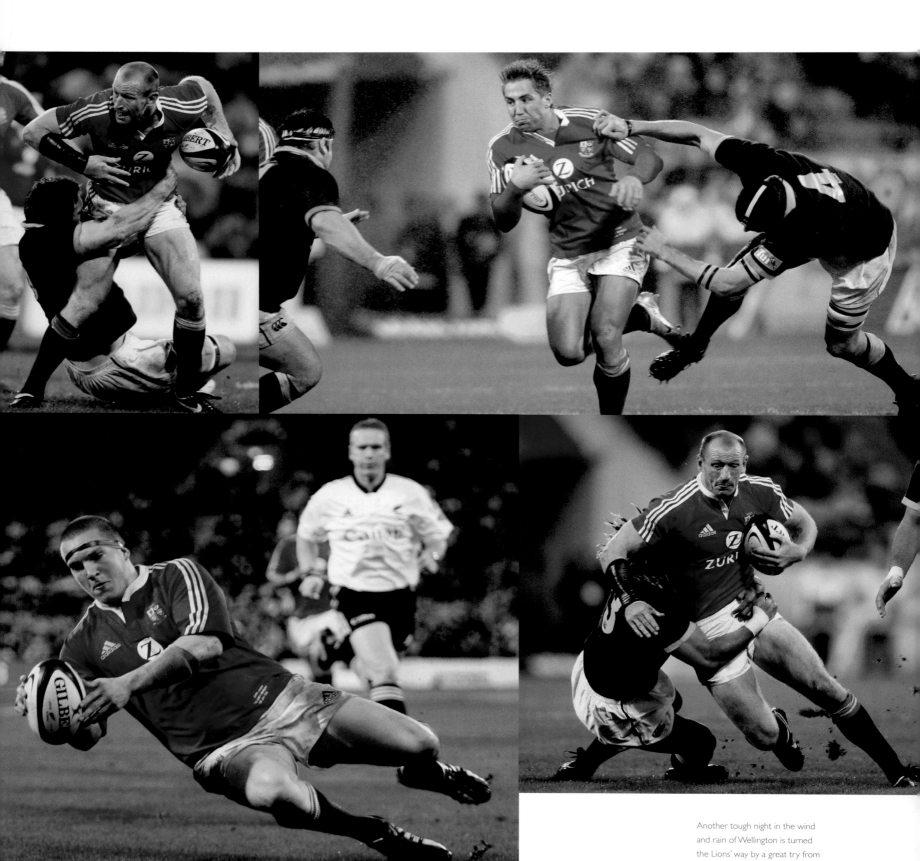

Another tough night in the wind and rain of Wellington is turned the Lions' way by a great try from man of the match Gethin Jenkins (*far left*)

Gareth Thomas caps a towering performance by powering through for a late try, before celebrating in his usual fashion

I'd like to say it was a dream come true to be selected for the Lions tour but, to be honest, that would be a lie as I never even dreamt I'd be in the squad. To make it was simply fantastic.

As a rugby player it doesn't get much better than winning a game in a Lions jersey, so to beat Wellington was brilliant. I never come off a rugby field totally happy with my performance, but it's fair to say I enjoyed that match. It's tough being away from home for so long, away from the family, but games like that make it all worthwhile.

To be honest, things had been getting tetchy in training in the run-up to the game and I think that did us a lot of good. Everyone was on everyone else's backs. After the Maori defeat people didn't want to accept anything but perfection.

We even decided to dispense with the traditional ceremony, whereby each Lions player is presented with his shirt the day before the game. Apart from the four lads who were making their debuts – Gareth Thomas, Jason Robinson, Simon Easterby and Neil Back – we decided that the rest of the jerseys would be waiting for us at the ground. After the defeat against the Maori, we wanted to make the statement that when we arrived at the Westpac Stadium we'd be ready to go against Wellington... and we were.

I thought every player stood up to be counted and the tour needed that. The team, the entire squad, all needed that performance. Statements were made at set-piece, at breakdown, in defence, in attack, everywhere.

The scrum went well, but I have to say the two props either side of me, Gethin Jenkins and Julian White, did some absolutely fantastic work – especially at the end when we weren't able to attack the scrum in the way we wanted to. There were times when we were getting penalised a lot, so we had to adapt our scrummaging. We couldn't attack the hit quite as much as we had been, so we had to be a little cuter and use a few tricks. Thankfully, referees can't see what's going on in the front row most of the time!

The boys reacted superbly. Gethin, in particular, showed he is eager. He's willing to get hands on the ball and he is great in defence. He's a real footballer and a guy who came of age on this trip.

There was a lot of talk about the breakdown on the tour and I was also very happy with the way that went against the Wellington number 7, who was battered and bruised by the end of the game. That is the greatest compliment we could be paid. It meant we were hitting the rucks hard and knocking them off the ball.

As each game on the tour went by every player was aware that Test selection was coming closer and closer. You had to try to make sure it didn't affect your performances. All you could do was make sure you did your job and take it from there. All I could do was my best on the field and hope I had done what I could to put my name forward.

As a team we just knew we had to make a step up against Wellington. We didn't need to pay any attention to all the talk in the press – we just knew we couldn't go on playing like we had against the Maori. We needed to make a statement of intent and that's exactly what we did.

Westpac Stadium
ATTENDANCE: 38,500

WELLINGTON 6		**LIONS 23**
Shannon Paku	15	Josh Lewsey (Shane Horgan, 68 mins)
Lome Fa'atau	14	Gareth Thomas
Ma'a Nonu	13	Brian O'Driscoll (Captain)
Tane Tuipulotu (Tamati Ellison, 77 mins)	12	Gavin Henson (Stephen Jones, 63 mins)
Roy Kinikinilau (Cory Jane, 78 mins)	11	Jason Robinson
Jimmy Gopperth	10	Jonny Wilkinson
Piri Weepu (Riki Flutey, 67 mins)	9	Dwayne Peel (Chris Cusiter, 72 mins)
Joe McDonnell (Captain)	1	Gethin Jenkins
Mahonri Schwalger (Luke Mahoney, 59 mins)	2	Shane Byrne
Tim Fairbrother (Mahonri Schwagler, 78 mins)	3	Julian White (Matt Stevens, 72 mins)
Luke Andrews	4	Danny Grewcock
Ross Filipo (Justin Purdie, 70 mins)	5	Ben Kay
Kristian Ormsby	6	Simon Easterby
Ben Herring (Kane Thompson, 41 mins)	7	Neil Back
Thomas Waldrom	8	Martin Corry (Vice Captain)

Replacements (unused): Gordon Bulloch, Richard Hill, Paul O'Connell, Lewis Moody

Tries: Jenkins, Thomas

Cons: Wilkinson 2

Pens: Gopperth 2   **Pens:** Wilkinson 3

Referee: Paul Honiss (New Zealand)

NEW ZEALAND 2005

THE
LIONS

The Lion Kings

jointhepride.co.uk

POWERING THE LIONS TOUR 2005

POWERADE

OFFICIAL SPORTS DRINK OF THE LIONS

ICE STORM

'Powerade' and 'Be Your Personal Best' are registered trade marks of The Coca-Cola Company.

Dunedin, Otago

Otago capital Dunedin is a city with a rich Scottish heritage, Dunedin actually being the old Gaelic name for Edinburgh. The area apparently reminded early settlers of the Midlothian countryside and the Otago rugby team is nicknamed The Highlanders

Wildlife Capital of New Zealand
DUNEDIN
NEW ZEALAND

www.DunedinNZ.com

MATCH 5

Otago
versus
British
& Irish Lions

Saturday June 18, 2005 at 7.10 pm, Carisbrook, Dunedin

$7.00

OFFICIAL
NEW ZEALAND LIONS SERIES 2005
PROGRAMME

NEW ZEALAND 2005

OTAGO v LIONS
18th JUNE 2005

With a week to go before the First Test in Christchurch, the Lions crossed Cook Strait to the South Island of New Zealand and headed for Dunedin, home of Otago and their notorious 'House of Pain' stadium. Otago have a formidable Lion-mauling pedigree, having beaten their illustrious opponents on no fewer than four occasions (in 1950, 1959, 1966 and 1993). Insisting Test places were still very much up for grabs, Sir Clive Woodward brought in Ryan Jones at number eight and gave Simon Easterby a shot at flanker. "I don't think for one minute the Test side has been picked yet," said Easterby, " so it has given those of us who are playing tomorrow a huge opportunity to show what we can do and push for that Test squad place."

The Lions fight back from 13-6 down in a bruising encounter at the 'House of Pain'

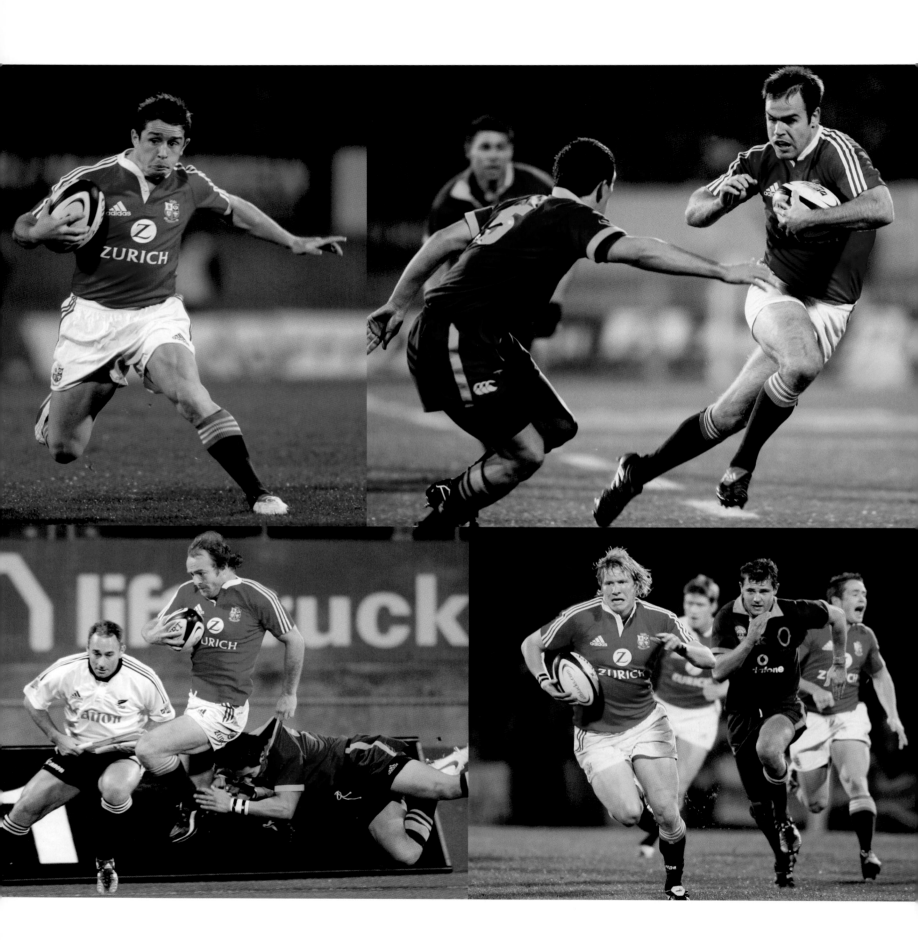

Another gruelling battle, the game is settled by a try by Ryan Jones, who continues his Welsh Grand Slam-winning form with a superb performance which includes an incredible 16 tackles

The night before my Lions debut against Otago my dad flew in to New Zealand and gave me a piece of advice that stayed with me all through the game. He said: "Son, have no regrets."

I took that philosophy onto the field and I hope I acquitted myself well. Having only arrived in the country the Monday before, after being called out to replace Simon Taylor, everything was a bit of a blur. One week I was getting ready to play for Wales in Canada, the next I had scored a try and taken part in a victory with the Lions. Incredible!

My dad was back in Wales when the call came through, so he and my mum jumped on a plane almost as quickly as I did. My mum and dad have been so important to me in my career, never pushing me but always giving me the encouragement I needed. After Wales' Grand Slam win I presented my dad with my Six Nations medal, but I think I'll be keeping my first Lions shirt.

Just having been part of a Lions tour is still sinking in. Playing for the Lions and scoring a try on my debut? That will take some time to assimilate and I might not be able to fully appreciate what I've done until I'm lying on a beach somewhere. As most people know, I was effectively out of work a year ago when the Celtic Warriors went to the wall. Luckily, I was picked up by the Ospreys before making my Wales debut in November. From there the fairytale season just went on and on. I really have been living the dream.

Against Otago, of course, there were things that could have gone better. But I came off the pitch knowing I couldn't have given any more and that is what I am looking for every time I play.

My philosophy is to give 100 per cent and have no regrets. Clive Woodward told us to look at ourselves in the mirror and be honest with ourselves. I wanted that Lions jersey so much, I wanted to be on that pitch so much, and I hope that came through in my performance.

I get exceptionally nervous before a game, so the hours before kick-off are always hard to cope with. In fact, I'd have every match kicking off at 10am if I could. Just wake up and get on the pitch. The worst is lunchtime. Your bags are packed and you're left just sitting in your room watching television, thinking "nine hours and it will all be over".

I am exactly the same as Neil Jenkins when it comes to nerves, which means that before kick-off I sometimes see my breakfast again! I'm nervous of under-performing and letting my team-mates and family down. I always worry about what people think.

In my short career with Wales, and now the Lions, I have found that, unlike when I am playing club rugby, all of a sudden I have 10 million armchair critics. There is nowhere to hide out there.

I always try and go into every match as if it will be my last, but that was easy against Otago because who knows where I will be by the time the next Lions tour comes around in four years time. I might not even be playing rugby. Being on the Lions tour has really hit home for me that you can never save anything for the next match. You can't worry about the next selection, because unless you deal with the match you're playing in the next one may never come.

Carisbrook
ATTENDANCE: 38,000

OTAGO 19		LIONS 30
Glen Horton	15	Geordan Murphy
Hayden Pedersen	14	Denis Hickie
Neil Brew (Jason Shoemark, 48 mins)	13	Will Greenwood (Vice Captain)
Seilala Mapusua	12	Gordan D'Arcy (Ollie Smith, 48 mins)
Matt Saunders	11	Shane Williams
Nick Evans	10	Charlie Hodgson (Ronan O'Gara, 70 mins)
Danny Lee (Chris Smylie, 75 mins)	9	Chris Cusiter (Matt Dawson, 61 mins)
Carl Hoeft	1	Graham Rowntree (Andrew Sheridan, 61 mins)
Jason MacDonald (Jed Vercoe, 53 mins)	2	Gordon Bulloch (Captain) (Steve Thompson, 61 mins)
Craig Dunlea (Jeremy Aldworth, 62 mins)	3	Matt Stevens
Fiipo Levi	4	Simon Shaw (Danny Grewcock, 61 mins)
Tom Donnelly	5	Donncha O'Callaghan
Craig Newby (Captain)	6	Simon Easterby
Josh Blackie (Alando Soakai, 78 mins)	7	Martyn Williams
Grant Webb	8	Ryan Jones (Michael Owen, 76 mins)

Replacements (unused): Andrew McClintock, Ryan Bambry

Try: Lee	**Tries:** Greenwood, Jones, S Williams
Con: Evans	**Cons:** Hodgson 3
Pens: Evans 3	**Pens:** Hodgson 3

REFEREE: Lyndon Bray (New Zealand)

GUINNESS®

Official Beer of the Lions 2005

Raise a glass to the 2005 Lions.

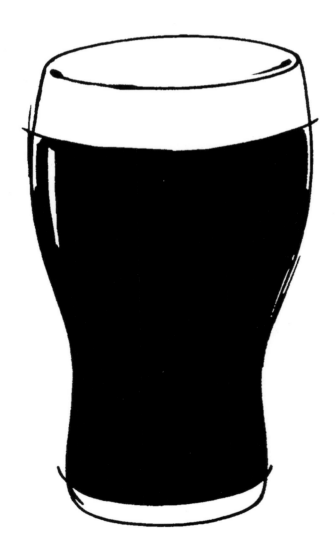

Invercargill, Southland

The southernmost city in New Zealand, Southland capital Invercargill has a reputation as 'the friendly city', with spectacular parks and the stunning Catlin coast within touching distance.

SOUTHLAND v LIONS

21st JUNE 2005

Situated right at the tip of the South Island, Rugby Park Stadium in Invercargill was to be the most southerly match venue of the tour and would also mark its halfway point. It was also the game where the Lions squad would divide into the midweek team under coach Ian McGeechan – soon to be christened the "Midweek Massive" – and the Test team. Consequently, news of Sir Clive Woodward's selection for the match against The Stags – hoping to emulate their solitary victory over the Lions in 1966 – was even more keenly awaited than usual. When the squad was announced all the attention was on the surprise selection of Wales star Gavin Henson, whom many had expected to make the First Test team. Henson said he was "devastated". Woodward insisted he was going for "experience" in the Test team, but also claimed the door was not necessarily closed to those picked to play against Southland. It was up to the players to prove him wrong.

SOUTHLAND NEW ZEALAND

After missing out on the First Test, the 'Midweek Massive' travelled south and emerged victorious again, despite Southland levelling the scores just after half-time

It was wonderful to score two tries against Southland, especially as they were my first for the Lions.

The game came at the end of a very tough week for the whole squad and it was remarkable how well the guys played.

It was a pivotal time for the tour. Two days earlier Clive Woodward had, for the first time on this trip, selected two sides at the same time: a team to travel to Invercargill for the Southland match and the other to stay in Christchurch to play in the First Test four days afterwards.

Along with many other players, I am sure, I was gutted to be named in the midweek team to play Southland, as all I had worked for was that Test jersey. It was really hard to take in because I thought I had a chance of making the Test side, or at least the 22. So to be told I wasn't involved came as such a shock.

I take my game very seriously and I thought it would take me a while to get over it. I hardly slept that night, it meant that much to me.

There are 45 players on tour and the coaches have to make the decisions in the end. I understand that. But it was very difficult for me to analyse exactly what was wrong with my game and what led to me being left out of the Test team. I felt I was playing quite well, especially off the back of that Grand Slam win with Wales. But I had a proper chat with Clive and he told me he didn't have a problem with the way I was playing – he just said that he wanted to go with experience for the Test.

It was tough because playing for the Lions means so much to me. It was a similar feeling to when I was left out of the World Cup in 2003. Back then I felt really low for ages, so this time I was determined to do all I could to make either the Second or Third Tests.

When all is said and done I just love playing rugby, so it was great to be able to get out on the pitch against Southland and get the disappointment out of my system. Having a game so quickly afterwards meant I could get straight back to what I do best. The worst thing would have been to just sit in a hotel room thinking about it. It was great to play 80 minutes and throw myself into rugby again.

I know Ian McGeechan said the Test selection would be reviewed after the game, but we all knew that, unless something dramatic happened, the 22 for Southland wouldn't be involved against New Zealand. That was tough for all of us to take, but the boys responded magnificently and showed the true spirit of the 2005 Lions.

Rugby Park Stadium
ATTENDANCE: 19,200

SOUTHLAND 16		LIONS 26
James Wilson	15	Geordan Murphy (Gordon D'Arcy, 76 mins)
Mana Harrison	14	Mark Cueto
Bryan Milne (Pehi Te Whare, 60 mins)	13	Ollie Smith (Tom Shanklin, 48 mins)
Faolua Muliaina	12	Gavin Henson
Watisoni Lotawa	11	Denis Hickie
Richard Apanui	10	Ronan O'Gara (Vice Captain)
Jimmy Cowan (Adam Clarke, 79 mins)	9	Gareth Cooper (Chris Cusiter, 49 mins)
Clarke Dermody (Captain)	1	Matt Stevens (Andrew Sheridan, 40 mins)
Jason Rutledge (David Hall, 57 mins)	2	Andy Titterrell (Gordon Bulloch, 48 mins)
Aarron Dempsey (Jayden Murch, 51 mins)	3	John Hayes
Hoani MacDonald	4	Simon Shaw
Daniel Quate	5	Donncha O'Callaghan
Hua Tamaraki (Rees Logan, 76 mins)	6	Lewis Moody
Hale T-Pole	7	Martyn Williams
Paul Miller (Jeff Wright, 38 mins)	8	Michael Owen (Captain) (Simon Easterby, 65 mins)

Replacement (unused): Matt Petre   **Replacement (unused):** Charlie Hodgson

Try: T-Pole   **Tries:** Henson 2

Con: Apanui   **Cons:** O'Gara 2

Pens: Apanui 3   **Pens:** O'Gara

REFEREE: Kelvin Deaker (Australia)

NEW ZEALAND 2005

ntl is proud to be
The Official Broadband Provider
to the British and Irish Lions 2005

Christchurch

Named after the cathedral college of Christ Church at Oxford University, Christchurch is officially the oldest city in New Zealand. The land is so flat that spectacular views can be obtained from almost any high building

ALL BLACKS V LIONS 1ST TEST

25th JUNE 2005

The moment of truth. Not since 1971 had the British & Irish Lions won the First Test of a series in New Zealand. Could they do it again? This was the question on the lips of the thousands upon thousands of Lions fans who poured into the city of Christchurch by plane, by camper van and even on an entire ship chartered just for the red army of British and Irish rugby fanatics. Sir Clive Woodward decided his best bet was to go with experience and his Test side – which included no fewer than eight of his 2003 World Cup-winning England team – had a combined international cap total of 696. Meanwhile, New Zealand coach Graham Henry voiced his concern that, despite a 91-0 victory over Fiji the night before the Lions went down to the Maori, his side would go into the match a little "under-cooked". Not even the heavy rain forecast for the night of the match was going to dampen the red hot atmosphere.

Sign of the times: New
Zealand is rugby mad
at the best of times,
but with the tour in
town Christchurch
goes Lions-crazy

The captain, Brian O'Driscoll, and the team's youngest player, Dwayne Peel, move forward to face *Ka-Mate, Ka-Mate,* the All Black haka, and accept the All Black challenge — a gesture wrongly interpreted as disrespectful by some sections of the local media

By now the population of New Zealand had been swelled by more than 20,000 Lions fans, and you don't come 15,000 miles not to have a good time!

Disaster strikes: First skipper Brian O'Driscoll, then Lions stalwart Richard Hill, are forced off the field – and out of the tour – within the first 20 minutes

One of my biggest regrets on this Lions tour is that we didn't give the fans the victories they deserved. They wanted something to go loopy over and we wanted to deliver it. I remember running out at the Gabba in 2001 and thinking "it doesn't get much better than this". But, once again, it was phenomenal. The support for these Lions tours is sensational. It is humbling to think about how much it has cost these supporters to come halfway around the world to follow us, how much time they must have taken off work.

We couldn't deliver a Test match victory for them, but I know I speak for every member of the playing and management team when I express my gratitude to those wonderful supporters.

The fans make the Lions experience what it is and it was probably in the First Test that their loyalty was stretched to the limit. We were suffering on the pitch in the terrible conditions, but they were out there in the open stands getting soaked through for most of the game.

The defeat in that game hurt me a lot. It is very painful to look back on. I took over the captaincy after Brian was injured, but I never felt this was my team. Even with Brian off the pitch it was his side, so I don't really regard myself as someone who has joined that exclusive band of Lions captains. I was just filling in.

And I really didn't take my chance. I don't think I had the impact on the game that I would have liked. These are games that stay with you for the rest of your life and I admit I am left with feelings of regret and disappointment.

I think Clive has gone on record saying that he would have liked to have played his Test side earlier and I think the fact that we hadn't played together was a big thing. For Test rugby you need to know each of your teammates' games inside out. Every player operates slightly differently to the next. When we bring the four nations together for the Lions, it is a wonderful thing. But it's tough and you need time to gel with the players around you. Having said that, we'd had eight or nine days to prepare as a Test team and I genuinely felt we could surprise and shock the All Blacks. This was an enormous game for us and we really wanted to produce our best rugby.

I know we lost our captain and Richard Hill inside the first 20 minutes, but during the game that didn't change my belief that we could win. Will Greenwood and Ryan Jones – both world-class players – came on to replace them, so I wouldn't want to use the injuries as an excuse. My reaction was, "OK - Brian's off - let's move on - we can still win". But, when you look back, they were killer blows. Although I'm not one for the "what ifs", the fact is they happened. But we didn't win the Test match, so we must move on.

The unfortunate thing was that I thought the All Blacks were very beatable. And the fact that we made a beatable side look very good is the biggest frustration of all. I always say that if you are going to lose a game then at least do it giving it your best shot, but we really didn't do that.

From the moment they lose captain Brian O'Driscoll, after 40 seconds, the Lions find themselves pinned back by a rampant New Zealand

Driving South Island rain and the loss of Richard Hill only add to the first half pressure

Rain man: Dwayne Peel stands firm
as the All Blacks defence closes in

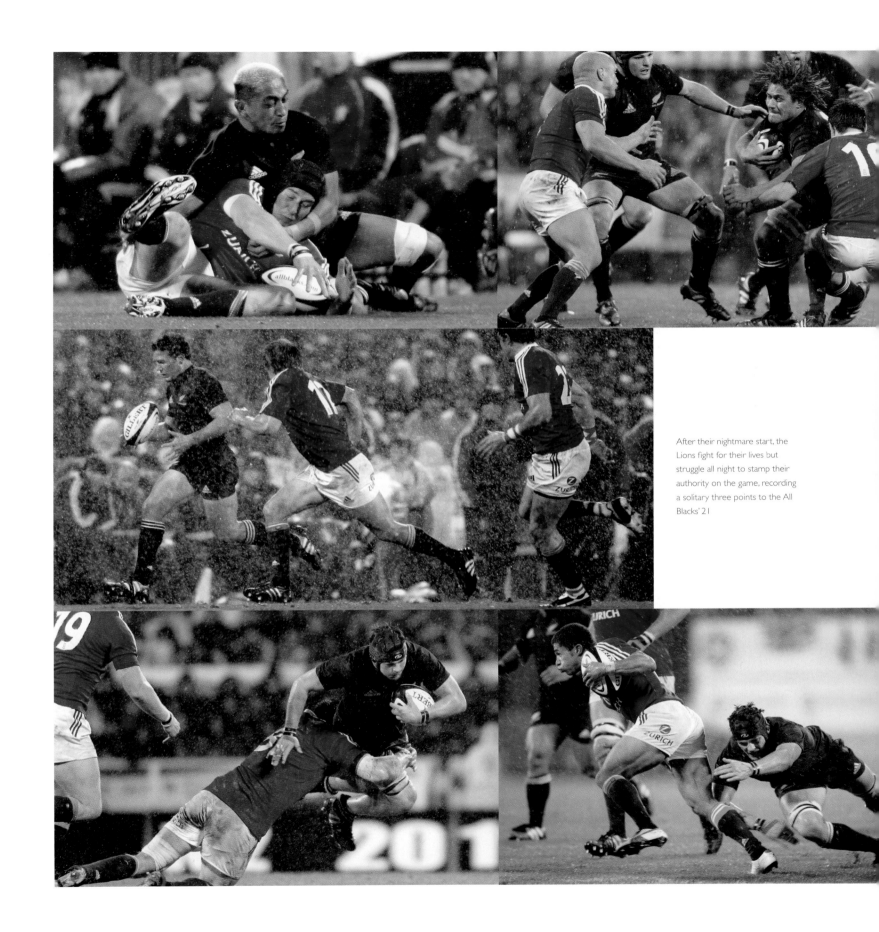

After their nightmare start, the
Lions fight for their lives but
struggle all night to stamp their
authority on the game, recording
a solitary three points to the All
Blacks' 21

As if defeat wasn't hard enough to take for the red legions, there was virtually no cover at Jade Stadium... not that the rain seemed to dampen the spirits of those dressed in black!

I know there was a lot of doom and gloom following this defeat, especially from outside the Lions camp, but I simply didn't buy into that sort of negative thinking.

Yes, we lost by 18 points and it was massively disappointing to lose the first of a three Test Series, but the gap between the two teams was not as big as people made out. The wind and the rain made it difficult, but at half time, only 11 points down, the mood in the dressing room was very positive and we believed we could haul them back.

Of course the injuries to Brian and Richard affected us. It would be great to say they didn't, but when a character like Brian leaves the field so early, and in the manner he did, it is bound to be a disruption. The fact that he wasn't carrying the ball when he was tackled did leave a bit of a sour taste in the mouth. Then after Brian departed we lost Richard Hill, a great international player and a great dog. They were two hammer blows.

But I don't think we lost heavily and we were a lot closer to the All Blacks than people gave us credit for. We leaked two tries, but I feel for large parts we contained them. We gave away a few key penalties when we didn't act coolly under pressure and in hindsight – which is a great little word in rugby – we would have acted differently.

We prepared really well and going into the game I was very confident of our basic skills. We trained very well during the week and the basics went well, but frustratingly they didn't during the game.

Nevertheless, I believe we put them under a lot more pressure than we were given credit for. That pressure was shown in the huge number of partial charge-downs. I have never played in, or seen, a game in which there have been so many, and in terms of where the ball went afterwards they had a bit of luck. I remember one kick deflected off a Lions hand and went straight to Tana Umaga, allowing him to head off down the field.

But, without doubt, they adapted far better to the conditions than us. They put a lot of ball in behind us and they played off the front foot better than we did.

On a personal level, I was brought in to do a job and to use my defensive leadership, and from that point of view it went pretty well. I thought we dealt pretty well with their attack, although obviously we were disappointed with Ali Williams' try from a line-out. That is a soft try to concede at any level.

Statistically the line-out was a nightmare. Doing the basics is crucial and we were found wanting there without question. But one thing that wasn't picked up on in the aftermath was that they often – illegally – had eight players in their line-out, sneaking an extra player in at the front when the referee was at the back and one at the back when the referee was at the front. It wasn't refereed and we didn't assist the referee in picking it up. No blame at his door because he can't see everything. We should have acted and dealt with it a lot better. They chanced their arm and got away with it.

Despite the defeat, the mood in the team after this match was one of resolve. We knew it would be crucial that we start well in Wellington.

Jade Stadium, Christchurch
ATTENDANCE: 37,200

ALL BLACKS 21		LIONS 3
Leon MacDonald (Mils Muliaina, 69 mins)	15	Jason Robinson (Shane Horgan, 57 mins)
Doug Howlett	14	Josh Lewsey
Tana Umaga (Captain) (Rico Gear, 74 mins)	13	Brian O'Driscoll (Captain) (Will Greenwood, 1 min)
Aaron Mauger	12	Jonny Wilkinson
Sitiveni Sivivatu	11	Gareth Thomas
Dan Carter	10	Stephen Jones
Justin Marshall (Byron Kelleher, 67 mins)	9	Dwayne Peel (Matt Dawson, 72 mins)
Tony Woodcock (Greg Somerville, 67 mins)	1	Gethin Jenkins
Keven Mealamu (Derren Whitcombe, 74 mins)	2	Shane Byrne (Steve Thompson, 57 mins)
Carl Hayman	3	Julian White
Chris Jack	4	Paul O'Connell
Ali Williams	5	Ben Kay (Danny Grewcock, 57 mins)
Jerry Collins (Sione Lauaki, 76 mins)	6	Richard Hill (Ryan Jones, 18 mins)
Richie McCaw	7	Neil Back
Rodney So'oialo	8	Martin Corry (Vice Captain)

Replacement (unused): Jonno Gibbes   **Replacement (unused):** Graham Rowntree

Tries: Williams, Sivivatu

Con: Carter

Pens: Carter 3   **Pen:** Wilkinson

Sin-bin: Paul O'Connell (11 mins)

REFEREE: Joël Jutge (France)

A Captain's Agony...

The morning after: His shoulder dislocated and his Lions dream shattered, Brian O'Driscoll struggles to come to terms with the events of the previous day, while Sir Clive Woodward highlights the tackle that ended his captain's tour.

Palmerston North, Manawatu

The Manawatu region is an outdoor pursuits paradise with attractions including jet boating, kayaking, gliding, 4WD safaris, fishing and hunting.

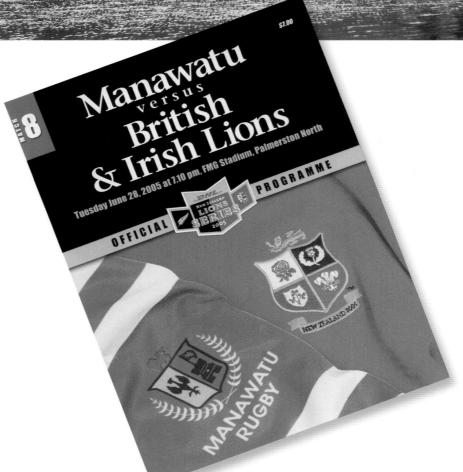

$7.00

MATCH 8

Manawatu
versus
British & Irish Lions

Tuesday June 28, 2005 at 7.10 pm, FMG Stadium, Palmerston North

NEW ZEALAND LIONS SERIES 2005

OFFICIAL PROGRAMME

NEW ZEALAND 2005

MANAWATU RUGBY

MANAWATU v LIONS

28th JUNE 2005

After the crushing disappointment of the First Test performance – not to mention the defeat – it was back to the North Island and a chance for the midweek team to restore some of that Lions pride. But the build-up to the Manawatu match was completely overshadowed by the furore over the tackle by All Blacks captain Tana Umaga, which dumped his Lions counterpart Brian O'Driscoll out of the tour. There were midnight press conferences, some angry banners and hastily printed T-shirts, and for a day or so it looked like the uplifting mood of the tour might turn nasty. But when the dust settled all the talk was of what changes the Lions would make for the Second Test, with much of the attention focusing on the dancing feet of Wales winger Shane Williams. Could he show the form against Manawatu that might make a difference in the Second Test?

Try and try again: The Lions' 17
tries are the perfect response
to the bitter disappointment of
the First Test

It was a make or break game for me against Manawatu. One Test had passed me by and with the second just four days after this game I simply had to impress. So when I came off the pitch with five tries under my belt I was feeling pretty happy.

I had worked really hard on the tour and I didn't let my head drop when I was left out of the First Test. I ran out onto the field against Manawatu knowing this was my chance and I don't believe I could have done any more to prove to Sir Clive Woodward that I was ready to face New Zealand.

In fact, five tries is the most I've ever scored in a match in my whole career. I did bag four for Wales in Japan four years ago, but never before have I managed five.

But there's no way this game was a one-man show. You don't score more than 100 points unless you perform as a whole. We put some good rugby together and it showed that we were mature enough to do that.

The coaching team of Ian McGeechan, Gareth Jenkins and Mike Ford ensured we had a great spirit in the midweek side. They asked us to play rugby with smiles on our faces and I think that was reflected in training and in the matches we played. We just loved to play rugby.

All the games on the tour were tough and it was fantastic to be involved in them. Part of the whole experience was facing up to the intensity of a tour to New Zealand. I don't think I've ever been to a country that loves rugby so much. Everywhere you go people come up to you to talk about rugby.

Every man, woman and child loves their rugby and with that comes its own pressure.

On the tour we didn't have that much time off, but we did have time for a quick trip to Queenstown to relax. I was one of those brave enough to do the bungee jump off the famous Queenstown Bridge, the site of the first ever bungee jump. Well we'd travelled all the way from Auckland, so I couldn't bottle out could I?

I learnt so much on the tour, both on and off the pitch. It was very memorable and, although I was only involved in one Test, I really enjoyed my time with the Lions. I think it could act as a real spur for my career and the careers of some of the other players on the trip. It will make me even more enthusiastic for my rugby with the Ospreys and Wales and I know that other players I have spoken to feel the same.

After a Lions tour you take the whole experience with you and I'm sure you can only go back home a better player.

Shane Williams

MANAWATU 6   LIONS 109

Frank Bryant	15	Geordan Murphy
Bevan Gray	14	Jason Robinson (Mark Cueto, 53 mins)
Jason Campbell	13	Ollie Smith
Matt Oldridge (Nick Buckley, 54 mins)	12	Gordon D'Arcy
Johnny Leota	11	Shane Williams
Graham Smith (Ben Trew, 47 mins)	10	Charlie Hodgson (Vice Captain) (Ronan O'Gara, 51 mins)
Jonathan Hargreaves (David Palu, 74 mins)	9	Chris Cusiter (Gareth Cooper, 40 mins)
Sam Moore	1	Andy Sheridan
Nathan Kemp (Captain)	2	Gordon Bulloch (Captain) (Andy Titterrell, 30 mins)
Keni Barrett (Isaac Cook, 46 mins)	3	John Hayes (Matt Stevens, 60 mins)
Tim Faleafaga	4	Simon Shaw
Paul Rodgers	5	Donncha O'Callaghan (Brent Cockbain, 40 mins)
Hayden Triggs (Chris Moke, 49 mins)	6	Martin Corry (Gordon Bulloch, 79 mins)
Josh Bradnock (Simon Easton, 77 mins)	7	Martyn Williams (Neil Back, 40 mins)
Bryan Matenga (Paula Maisiri, 49 mins)	8	Michael Owen

Tries: S Williams 5, Corry, Murphy, Robinson, Hodgson, Smith, Back, D'Arcy, O'Gara 2, Cueto 2, Cooper

Cons: Hodgson 7, O'Gara 5

Pens: Hargreaves 2

Sin-bin: Kemp (29 mins), Easton (80 mins)   **Sin-bin:** Stevens (74 mins)

REFEREE: Lyndon Bray (New Zealand)

TENSION ✓
DESPAIR ✓
ELATION ✓

SURE FOR MEN. IT WON'T LET YOU DOWN DURING THE LIONS TOUR.

Official Partner of the Lions.

Wellington

The arts and culture capital of New Zealand, Wellington is just two kilometres wide making it easily explored on foot.

ALL BLACKS v LIONS 2ND TEST

2nd JULY 2005

With 17 midweek tries to give the squad a lift, the Lions returned to Wellington for the Second Test, with Sir Clive Woodward vowing: "It's time to shake things up". Knowing that only victory in the Westpac Stadium would save the Series, the Lions boss made seven changes to his First Test team, bringing in centre Gavin Henson, five-try man Shane Williams, forwards Steve Thompson & Donncha O'Callaghan and a back row trio of Simon Easterby, Lewis Moody and Ryan Jones. The pressure was mounting and, having appointed the "inspirational" Gareth Thomas as his new Test captain, on the eve of the match Woodward told the assembled media: "I promise you there will be a completely different show come Saturday night."

They might be 1-0 down in the Series, but you wouldn't know it as the Lions party descends on Wellington

No doubt where their loyalties lie!

The words of the awe-inspiring All
Black haka, *Ka mate, ka mate, ka ora,
ka ora*, means, *Tis death, tis death, tis
life, tis life*

What a start! Gareth Thomas finds a gap
from nowhere and sensationally puts the
Lions ahead with 1 minute, 33 seconds
on the clock

Alfie's try gets a hug from
hooker Thompson on the pitch...
and the royal seal of approval
from Prince William in the stands

The Lions' fans are in dreamland...

... until Tana Umaga and Sitiveni Sivivatu bring them crashing down to earth with first half replies

(*Overleaf*) Paul O'Connell epitomises the team spirit as the Lions try to force their way back into the game

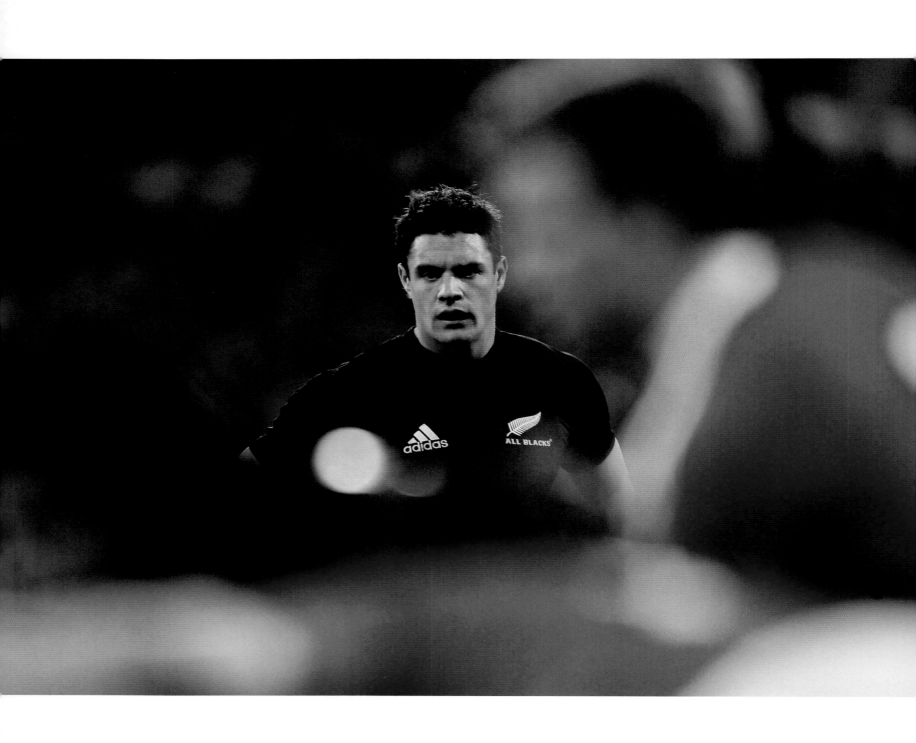

If Dan Carter announced his arrival on the international rugby scene in the First Test, in the Second he conquers it with a masterclass in outside half play which sees him score two tries, five penalties and four conversions in an incredible 33 point performance

But the Lions don't give up the Series without one hell of a fight, and the final scoreline does not reflect the fact that they had the mighty All Blacks under serious pressure for long spells of the match

Like every other player in Britain and Ireland, I dreamt of one day playing for the Lions in a Test match. But I would happily have sat in the stands in Wellington in exchange for a Series victory.

My late try was little or no compensation for the Second Test defeat and even though we showed a marked improvement from the performance in the First Test we still didn't win. At this level winning is everything. In this game no-one remembers the losers.

When I came on the tour as a replacement for Lawrence Dallaglio I wasn't expecting anything. To make the Test side was fantastic, but I would have given all that up for a Lions victory in the series. That would have been unbelievable.

I got my chance in the Test side when Richard Hill was injured in Christchurch. Richard was still on crutches when the Second Test came around, but he still took the trouble to seek me out to give me some words of encouragement, and I really appreciated that from someone I respect so much.

We could take something from parts of our performance in the Second Test. But as much as we stepped up from our performance in the First Test, so New Zealand raised the bar as well.

The scoreline suggests we got well beaten, but I think it flatters them a little. They were undoubtedly the better side, but I can't accept they were 30 points better than us.

Like any game the match hinged on several key moments. We gave up soft points at crucial stages of the game. As soon as we scored, we seemed to concede. That took away any momentum we had built up.

But there were times when we thought it was going very well. Even at 21-13 at half-time we were still in it, but then they scored just after the break, which meant we had to chase the game a little.

The big challenge for Lions tours is to come together and gel. I think it is very significant that New Zealand had been together as a team for a long time. They carried on the form they showed at the end of last season in that big win over France. They are very strong. You have to put them down early and when we didn't do that they attacked from anywhere. Their counter-attack was fantastic and something we must learn from.

The All Blacks have an exceptional bunch of players. They can all run with the ball and they are very good on their feet. If we slipped off tackles their ability to off-load was better than any side I have ever come across. I don't know what you put that down to, but we can all learn something from it and hopefully try to emulate it.

It's agony on the pitch, and in the stands, as 1-0 in the Series becomes an irretrievable 2-0...

Me and the boys were devastated to lose the Test Series, but I was far from devastated by the way the team played. I was so proud of the performance they put in.

After the game someone asked me whether leading out the Lions was my proudest moment. In fact, my proudest moment was leading them off the field because we had made a pledge to each other that we wouldn't make the same mistakes as we did in the First Test.

We promised each other we would not come off thinking "what if"'. So the boys walked off the field knowing they had given everything they had and there was nothing more we could have done to overcome this New Zealand team.

I know people will point to a 30 point defeat, but the scoreboard is irrelevant to me because I am really proud of the way we dealt with the defeat. I don't fear failure and I don't fear losing. I fear not trying and not for one minute of the 80 did the boys stop trying.

For that reason, I don't know if I will ever get over the First Test defeat in Christchurch. We played so poorly. But I will easily get over this one because we gave it our best shot and we never gave up.

Before the game we really needed to show the New Zealanders that we were there to play rugby and set them a challenge. We did that by making a fabulous start and for the first ten minutes we were on top of them. Unfortunately a game of rugby lasts 80!

But I never felt the game was slipping away from us and I don't think the match suggests a gap between the northern and southern hemispheres. I think it is pretty obvious that New Zealand are the best team in the world at the moment and Dan Carter was sensational - what a player. But they are lethal from 1 to 22. They are bringing on subs that are world-class.

The All Blacks probably played the perfect game in Wellington. The guys gave everything and we got great passion and pride from our performance. But as soon as you lose the ball against this side you are looking at going back 80 metres or conceding seven points.

It has taken three or four years to get Wales playing the way we did during the Six Nations. To do it in three to four weeks is pretty much an impossibility. But that is the magic of the Lions. It's all about getting together and knuckling down. And even in the last minute of the Second Test the guys were still believing. Obviously not believing they could win, but believing in each other.

After the game the changing room was silent, as the boys were devastated to lose. I don't care what people read into the scoreline, we went out there to try our best. From 1 to 22 the guys gave everything they had. On the day we just weren't good enough.

Wetspac Stadium, Wellington
ATTENDANCE: 37,000

ALL BLACKS 48   LIONS 18

Mils Muliaina	15	Josh Lewsey
Rico Gear	14	Jason Robinson
Tana Umaga (Captain)	13	Gareth Thomas (Captain)
Aaron Mauger (Leon MacDonald, 38 mins)	12	Gavin Henson (Shane Horgan, 70 mins)
Sitiveni Sivivatu (Ma'a Nonu, 73 mins)	11	Shane Williams
Dan Carter	10	Jonny Wilkinson (Stephen Jones, 60 mins)
Byron Kelleher (Justin Marshall, 66 mins)	9	Dwayne Peel
Tony Woodcock (Campbell Johnstone, 78 mins)	1	Gethin Jenkins (Graham Rowntree, 60 mins)
Keven Mealamu (Derren Whitcombe, 70 mins)	2	Steve Thompson (Vice Captain) (Shane Byrne, 78 mins)
Greg Somerville	3	Julian White (Graham Rowntree, 61-66 mins)
Chris Jack (Jono Gibbes, 74 mins)	4	Paul O'Connell
Ali Williams	5	Donncha O'Callaghan (Martin Corry, 73 mins)
Jerry Collins (Sione Lauaki, 66 mins)	6	Simon Easterby
Richie McCaw	7	Lewis Moody
Rodney So'oialo	8	Ryan Jones

Replacements (unused) Martyn Williams, Matt Dawson

Tries: Carter 2, Umaga, Sivivatu, McCaw   **Tries:** Thomas, Easterby

Cons: Carter 4   **Con:** Wilkinson

Pens: Carter 5   **Pens:** Wilkinson 2

REFEREE: Andrew Cole (Australia)

Sign Here Please...

The Lions players embark on a shirt-signing session at the team hotel

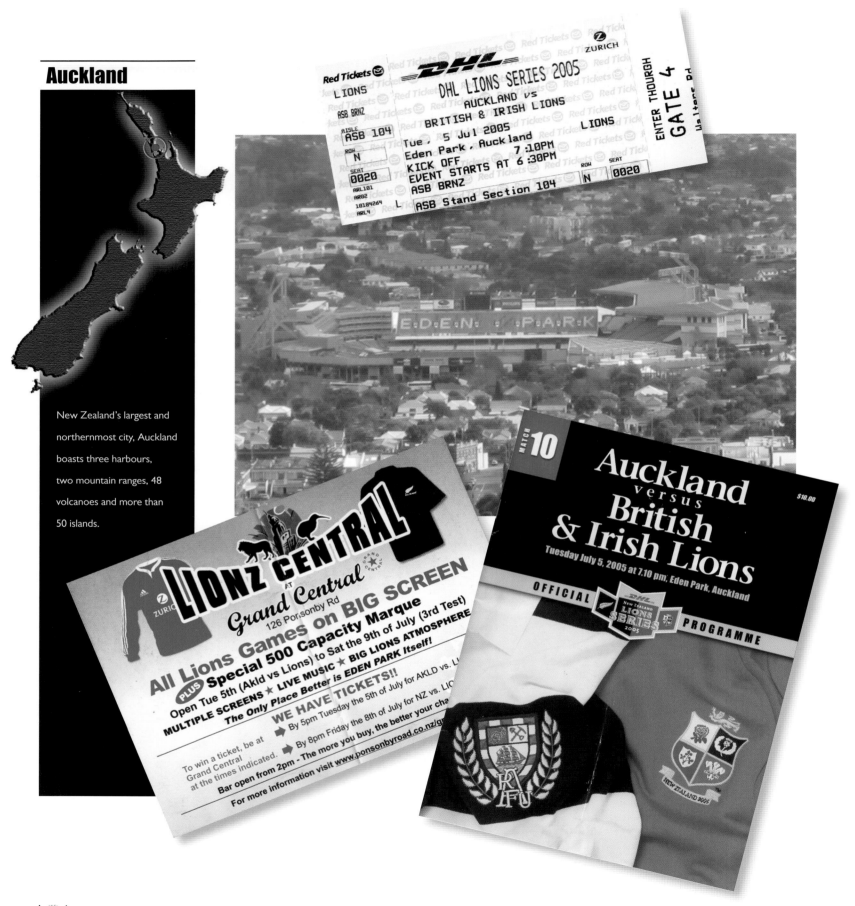

Auckland

New Zealand's largest and northernmost city, Auckland boasts three harbours, two mountain ranges, 48 volcanoes and more than 50 islands.

Red Tickets

LIONS

ASB BRNZ

AISLE ASB 104

ROW N

SEAT 0020

ARL101
AR02
10104264
ARL4

L

ENTER THOURGH GATE 4

DHL LIONS SERIES 2005
AUCKLAND Vs
BRITISH & IRISH LIONS
Tue, 5 Jul 2005
Eden Park, Auckland
KICK OFF   7:10PM
EVENT STARTS AT 6:30PM
ASB BRNZ
ASB Stand Section 104

ROW N

SEAT 0020

LIONS

LIONZ CENTRAL
AT
Grand Central
126 Ponsonby Rd

All Lions Games on BIG SCREEN
PLUS Special 500 Capacity Marque
Open Tue 5th (Akld vs Lions) to Sat the 9th of July (3rd Test)
MULTIPLE SCREENS ★ LIVE MUSIC ★ BIG LIONS ATMOSPHERE
The Only Place Better is EDEN PARK itself!

WE HAVE TICKETS!!
➡ By 5pm Tuesday the 5th of July for AKLD vs. LI
➡ By 8pm Friday the 8th of July for NZ vs. LIO
➡ By 2pm - The more you buy, the better your cha

To win a ticket, be at Grand Central at the times indicated.

Bar open from 2pm
For more information visit www.ponsonbyroad.co.nz/gr

MATCH 10

$10.00

Auckland
VERSUS
British & Irish Lions
Tuesday July 5, 2005 at 7.10 pm, Eden Park, Auckland

OFFICIAL

NEW ZEALAND LIONS SERIES 2005

PROGRAMME

NEW ZEALAND 2005

AUCKLAND v LIONS

5th JULY 2005

With the Test series gone, it was down to Ian McGeechan's men to keep the Lions flag flying. With four midweek victories in four matches, it was on to Third Test venue, Auckland, to face the local provincial side for by far their toughest test yet. Not only does Auckland possess the best record of any New Zealand provincial team against the Lions, with an amazing six wins and a draw, but their team would include All Blacks Joe Rokocoko, Sam Tuitupou, Steve Devine and Brad Mika. The significance of the match was not lost on the legions of Lions fans streaming into the city determined to keep the party in full swing, despite their disappointment at losing the Series. By now the local papers were raving about the exemplary behaviour of the visiting supporters.

After the Second Test the *Wellington Dominion* wrote: "Some didn't even seem to know the result, as they welcomed yesterday morning with an undefeatable blaze of red shirts, Union Jacks and chants of '*Lions, Lions, Lions*'."

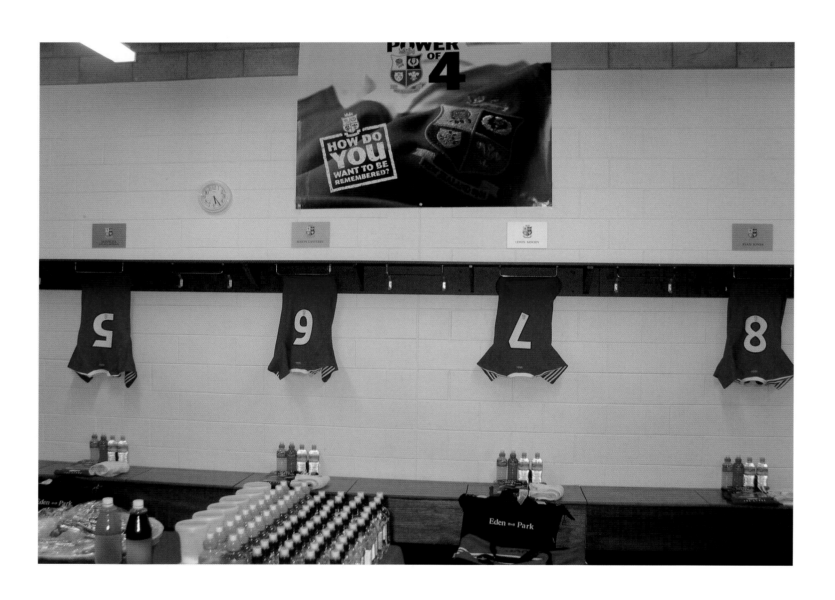

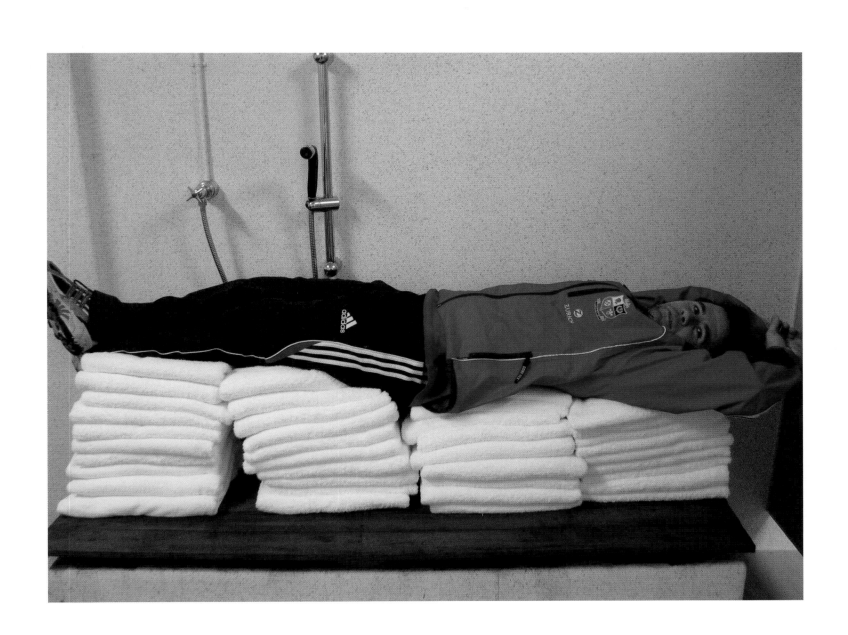

The calm before the storm: Fitness
coach Craig White thoughtfully
warms up the players' towels

Provincial heavyweights Auckland live up to their billing as the Midweek Massive's toughest test and the match proves to be a titanic struggle, with the Lions holding out for victory by four points

Ben Kay (*above*) bears the marks
of battle, while Matt Stevens (*right*)
shows the determination required
to win all five midweek matches in
the rugby hotbeds of New Zealand.

It was fantastic for the 'Midweek Massive' to finish the tour unbeaten. Sitting in the changing room afterwards, the boys were acknowledging it was a big win. We had focused really hard on this game since selection at the weekend. This was our Test match.

For all those players who were involved in the midweek games it was a very satisfying end to the tour. A great team spirit had built up within the whole Lions squad and, as we saw with the celebrations in the changing room after the game, the whole tour party was chuffed to bits that we went undefeated.

Losing the Test Series hurt all of us, but this was a huge lift. It would have been easy for people to write us off, but we sent a message as a squad that we would be taking the final Test very seriously indeed.

It was a big game for me and a big game for all the boys. Personally, I wasn't out there to prove a point to anyone but myself. Yes, I wanted to be starting in the Test team. I wanted the number nine on my back. I don't want to be finishing my career on the bench. But I am a team player and I hope my team-mates think I am a team player.

I will only play well if the forward pack play well and in this game they were pretty outstanding. They put Auckland under pressure and that made mine, Charlie [Hodgson] and Rog's [Ronan O'Gara] lives an awful lot easier.

I've experienced all the highs and the lows of Lions rugby and that's what makes characters out of us all. I think people will remember this trip for the right reasons and especially the 'Midweek Massive', a phrase coined by tour doctor Gary O'Driscoll. When they are back home playing for their clubs or in the Six Nations, the players will remember, with a glint in the eye, that they were a part of this team.

As with every Lions tour people will soon start looking for lessons that can be learnt for next time. One thing that has definitely worked in 2005 is the concept of two coaching teams: one for the Saturday side and one for the midweek side.

The midweek coaching team of Ian McGeechan, Gareth Jenkins and Mike Ford played a massive role in creating the spirit. You've got a huge amount of experience in Geech. He pitched it superbly well. Geech was a Lions head coach and many people wouldn't have been able to handle going from that to coaching the midweek side, but he enjoyed it. Gareth Jenkins is one of the most passionate rugby men I have ever met. All of the squad have nothing but great words to say about those guys.

The focus of a Lions tour has got to be success in the Tests. But to have won every midweek game and to have done that in New Zealand, where rugby is a religion and every game is so intense, is an immense achievement that the coaching staff and all the players are rightly proud of.

Matt Dawson

Flying Lion: Mark Cueto *(far left)* gets airborne.

English warhorses Matt Dawson and Graham Rowntree *(above left)* congratulate each other on another international rugby achievement while Brent Cockbain and Gordon D'Arcy *(above right)* celebrate with the fans

It was a special honour for me to captain the side dubbed the 'Midweek Massive'. Then to finish with a victory which made us unbeaten on the tour was some achievement.

I was lucky enough to captain the side three times – against Otago, Manawatu and Auckland – and it was great to come away from the tour saying I had captained the Lions in three victories. The Auckland game was by far our toughest on the trip, as they had a side packed with Super 12 players, and it says a lot for our spirit that we managed to complete another win.

For many players it was hard being selected for the midweek side time and time again. Many of these guys are used to being first picks for their clubs, or in some cases their countries, and I think it says a lot for them that we didn't have any cases of guys "going off tour".

It proved, in many ways, what great coaches we had in Ian McGeechan, Gareth Jenkins, Mike Ford and Craig White. They created a side from nothing and brought a real attitude to it. They drilled into us the attitude that once you take the field in that famous jersey you need to show it the respect it deserves and perform to your very best, whether you're playing a Test match or a game against Manawatu.

My final week on tour started with the great win over Auckland and ended in unexpected fashion when I picked up a Lions cap against New Zealand.

Steve Thompson had originally been selected to start the Third Test, with Shane Byrne on the bench, so I had headed off to Queenstown on the Thursday for some much needed R&R.

After we got back to Auckland some of the midweek team were heading out for a few beers on the Friday and they invited me. But I decided on a quiet one. I was so glad I had that 'quiet one' when Clive told me on Saturday morning that Steve was out with illness and I was on the bench.

That spot on the bench turned into eight minutes of action on the field and I gather my appearance on the field even prompted a chorus of 'Flower of Scotland' in the Eden Park press box.

Apart from winning, Lions tours are about friendships and getting to know new people. The guys you may have played against for club and country turn from foes into friends. I suppose, for me, the guys who I packed down with like Graham Rowntree, Matt Stevens and Donncha O'Callaghan are the ones I got to know best, but everyone who played in that midweek team got on pretty well.

We lost the Test series 3-0, so I'm not sure there will be too many reunion dinners of the Class of 2005. Nonetheless, I'll continue the friendships I forged and will fondly remember the good and the bad times from our trip to New Zealand. I made a lot of friends on the Lions tour of 2005 and I didn't make a single enemy.

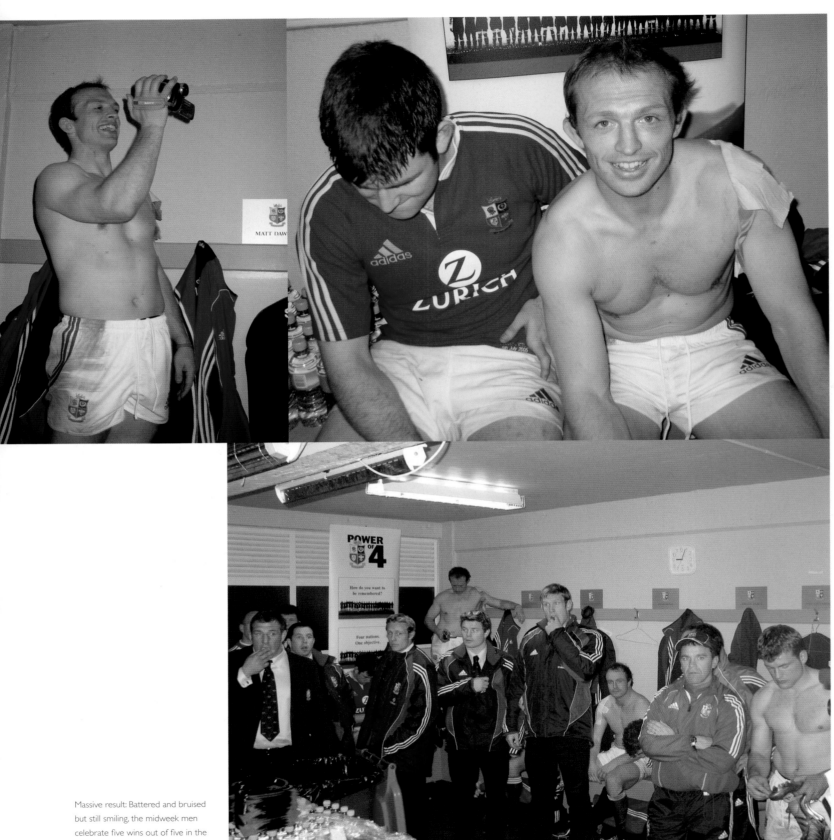

Massive result: Battered and bruised
but still smiling, the midweek men
celebrate five wins out of five in the
Eden Park dressing room

V LIONS

Four nations, five wins!

Eden Park
ATTENDANCE: 47,500

AUCKLAND 13   LIONS 17

Brent Ward	15	Geordan Murphy
Isa Nacewa (Gavin Williams, 70 mins)	14	Mark Cueto
Ben Atiga (Isaia Toe'ava, 76 mins)	13	Will Greenwood (Shane Horgan, 48 mins)
Sam Tuitupou	12	Gordon D'Arcy
Joe Rokocoko	11	Denis Hickie
Tasesa Lavea	10	Charlie Hodgson (Vice Captain) (Ronan O'Gara, 20 mins)
Steve Devine	9	Matt Dawson
Saimone Taumoepeau (Chris Heard, 60 mins)	1	Graham Rowntree
Semisi Telefon (John Fonokalati, 76 mins)	2	Gordon Bulloch (Captain)
John Afoa	3	John Hayes (Matt Stevens, 59 mins)
Brad Mika (Jermone Kaino, 45 mins)	4	Simon Shaw
Bryce Williams	5	Ben Kay (Brent Cockbain, 35 mins)
Justin Collins (Captain)	6	Jason White (Martin Corry, 54 mins)
Daniel Braid	7	Martyn Williams
Angus MacDonald (Kurtis Haiu, 67 mins)	8	Michael Owen

Replacement (unused): Tanela Moa   **Replacements (unused):** Andy Titterell, Chris Cusiter

Try: Nacewa   **Try:** M Williams

Con: Ward   **Pens:** Hodgson, O'Gara 3

Pens: Ward 2

REFEREE: Steve Walsh (New Zealand)

NEW ZEALAND 2005

Pride of place

Proud to be Official Sponsor
of the British & Irish Lions 2005

Too Many Cooks!

Tour chef Dave Campbell enlists the 'help' of some
of the players in cooking dinner for the whole squad.
Somewhat stereotypically, Donncha O'Callaghan and
Simon Easterby are put in charge of potatoes, while
Josh Lewsey prepares his special recipe mushy peas

Auckland

In the Maori language Auckland is known as Tamaki-makau-rau, which translates as 'the maiden with a hundred lovers'.

ALL BLACKS
V LIONS 3RD TEST

9th JULY 2005

After the euphoria of victory over Auckland, on the eve of the Final Test the mood of the tour was shattered as news of the terrorist bombings in London filtered through to the bars and clubs of Auckland. All over the city Lions fans were to be found glued to TV screens, disbelieving, and frantically trying to get through to friends and relatives back home (NZ phone companies later offered free credit to Lions fans who had been using their phones at this time). For many it was the only quiet night of the tour. All Blacks coach Graham Henry summed up the mood the following day when he said: "The game really doesn't seem that significant when these sorts of things are going on in the world." But as kick-off approached, the mood changed to one of solidarity and defiance. The unspoken feeling was that the best way to answer the terrorists was to get back to normal and play a Test Match... although hopefully with a different scoreline this time!

Down but not out: Widely praised for their great humour and immaculate behaviour, not to mention their contribution to the New Zealand economy, the red army descends on Auckland

The buoyant atmosphere of the tour is momentarily shattered when news of the terrorist attacks on London reaches the bars and hotels of Auckland... but by the time Eden Park rises as one to observe a minute's silence the mood is one of defiant pride

We are not afraid: No terrorist is going to stop this way of life!

The Lions come flying out of the blocks to race into a 6-0 lead, only for Conrad Smith (*right*) to scythe through their defence and bring the All Blacks right back into it

Ali Williams scores in controversial circumstances and Umaga goes over twice in the second half, the All Blacks once again getting points on the board during the crucial phases of the match

When the Lions went to Australia in 2001 I still hadn't played a game of professional rugby – I watched the tour on TV – so to end this trip having made my Lions Test debut is something very special, especially having not made the original 44-man squad.

The Series had been lost, but the experience was incredible and it has definitely increased my hunger to get on the trip to South Africa in four years time. I'm young enough for the next tour and it is something I will target.

Coming from a background in football, having only taken up rugby when I was 19, I think it meant I wasn't under as much pressure as many of the other players. I know more about the game now than I did, but my lack of historical knowledge compared to the likes of Gavin Henson took the pressure off. The less I knew about the history of the Lions, and what it meant to tour New Zealand, the less pressure I put on myself.

After missing the first two Tests I had pretty much put the third out of my mind. Approaching the midweek game against Auckland as my last on this trip, I said to myself: "It's the last game of the season, so give it a good crack". That's the way it was. You just had to keep going. You couldn't moan and groan about selection. The quality of players in the Lions squad spoke for itself. No one could expect to be on the team sheet. You had to work for that and then take your chance when it came.

So when I got the nod from Clive for the Third Test it was fantastic. To be honest, I couldn't have imagined playing in a Lions Test this time last year, but things have really taken off and I hope people will say that my rugby came on during the tour. I certainly felt I got more involved in other duties than I have before and I even got the chance to send out a few touch finders. Some people didn't even know I had a left boot!

In all the matches I played I felt confident enough to come off my wing – especially against Auckland – and go looking for work. I only hope the progress I have made with the Lions will continue when I kick off the new season for the Sale Sharks.

But it wasn't just my career that took off in New Zealand. One day we went off-roading and it was very nearly the end of more than just the tour for me and my passenger, Josh Lewsey. We took a turn down what looked like a pretty easy track when, suddenly, we were halfway up a hill with a 50ft drop just outside the window. The wheels started to slip away, I slammed the brakes on and if it hadn't been for a wire fence we'd have been over and out. We had to be winched to safety. We nearly lost more than the Test Series!

Woodward turns to his old stalwart Matt Dawson for some inspiration, and the Lions continue to fight to the last

Rico Gear is congratulated by his
captain, Tana Umaga, after the All
Black winger's late try shatters any
hopes of a late Lions revival

Battered but unbowed: Lions prop
Graham Rowntree

The realisation of a 3-0 Series defeat…

Before you go on your first Lions tour every player talks about what a great honour it is and how the trip is the pinnacle of your career. But, to be honest, I had no idea how special pulling on that red jersey is until I had done it.

I'd never held the Lions in as high esteem as some but, having experienced it, I do now. I now have a better understanding of the history and tradition that goes with this great team and that was helped by the involvement of people like Gareth Jenkins and Ian McGeechan. It meant so much to all the players.

In the professional era a season can go by in a whirl. We move from one big game to another. In the run-up to the Lions tour I was playing in the Six Nations, then the semi-finals of the Heineken Cup, followed by a trip to Twickenham for the Zurich Premiership Final. That fast-paced season means that, although I was delighted to win my place in the Lions squad, I didn't have time for it to sink in – and perhaps it won't properly sink in for quite a while yet.

I had dreamed about scoring the final try in the final Test to win the Series 2-1 for the Lions. Well, I managed the first bit by scoring the Lions' final try, but unfortunately the rest of the dream didn't come true. It wasn't a particularly glamorous score in the end, driven over by the pack, but it was great to get over the line and actually score for the Lions. At that point we only needed two converted tries, so the boys still felt we had a way back into the match.

But, perhaps because we lost, my greatest memories of this tour will be of the friendships I gained and the little events off the field, like seeing my great friend Geordan Murphy do a bungee jump off the Sky Tower in Auckland. And, no, I didn't follow him, as heights aren't my strong point. Nowadays we rarely get the chance to mix with opposing players after matches, so it was great to get to know people like Michael Owen, Ryan Jones and Ronan O'Gara, and I'll never forget the humour of guys like Donncha O'Callaghan and Denis Hickie.

Everyone has talked about the spirit of the Lions of 2005 and I think it was best summed up by the reaction of those players who weren't selected for the final Test. Clive had decided to let all those not selected head down to Queenstown for some much-needed R&R, but we still needed eight of them to stay behind for training. After he announced the team, Clive asked for volunteers to stay back and train with the Test team. A thankless task, you might think. But when the question went out no-one shirked it and the hands shot up. We had far more than eight volunteers. That showed how united the squad was. Even though we had already lost the Series 2-0, we so badly wanted to win the Third Test.

We started the game really well, but then found ourselves in the incredible position of conceding 14 points while they had Tana Umaga in the sin bin. When Tana was sin-binned I thought 'happy days', but a couple of lapses in concentration later and we were behind. In many ways those tries summed up the series, in that the All Blacks seemed to take every opportunity that came their way. Whenever we made a mistake they capitalised on it.

The dream is over

I know that the future of the Lions has been questioned in some quarters, but I hope this tour has proved that the side has a big role to play in professional rugby.

Yes, we lost the Series 3-0, but that shouldn't detract from the impact this Lions tour has had in New Zealand and in the rest of the rugby world.

I sincerely hope there are other tours. I thoroughly enjoyed it and would love to think I'll still be around challenging for a place in four years' time, when the next group of Lions are about to board the plane to South Africa.

Growing up in south Wales I can remember hearing tales of the Lions from relatives who were lucky to be around in the 1970s when they last went to New Zealand and won. I grew up in awe of the Lions and, yes, I can confirm it is as special as you think. The jersey means as much to the players as it ever did.

Overall it was a really enjoyable tour. We were spoilt and given everything we needed to succeed. The organisation was brilliant and the camaraderie was awesome. There were no cliques and everyone gave 100 per cent, which is all anyone can ask for.

On the pitch we clearly could have been a little more efficient and we could have shown a little more, but there is no point in having regrets. The rugby was hard, as we always knew it would be in New Zealand, but ultimately that is what it is all about - testing yourself against the best.

I'm not making any excuses, but we were hit pretty hard with injuries. Eleven, twelve, thirteen players probably had just one training run together before the start of the First Test. The nucleus of the New Zealand side was very familiar with its game plan and perhaps that's where they had the edge. We had to establish a similar game plan and get used to it very quickly.

For me, the key on this tour has been the contact area. I am normally in a position for a great view of it and I was so impressed with the efficiency of the All Blacks. We have to look at our technique to make sure we get the right numbers there. Whoever controls the breakdown controls the match and you have to give New Zealand credit for the way they dominated that area on the tour.

I have just finished the longest season of my life, with the French Championship ending in June and then the Lions tour, but it has been the most enjoyable. To finish in New Zealand with three Tests has been hard, but I've never learnt more from a season than this one.

What you discover on a tour like this are your weaknesses. So, for myself and the rest of the squad, we now have things to go away and work on in becoming better players. I hope the Lions tour will act as a spur for my career. It has certainly inspired and challenged me to go away and improve.

Stephen Jones

ALL BLACKS 38   LIONS 19

Mils Muliaina	15	Geordan Murphy (Ronan O'Gara, 66 mins)
Rico Gear	14	Mark Cueto
Conrad Smith	13	Will Greenwood
Tana Umaga (Captain)	12	Gareth Thomas (Captain) (Shane Horgan, 51 mins)
Sitiveni Sivivatu	11	Josh Lewsey
Luke McAlister	10	Stephen Jones
Byron Kelleher (Justin Marshall, 76 mins)	9	Dwayne Peel (Matt Dawson, 48 mins)
Tony Woodcock (Campbell Johnstone, 54 mins)	1	Gethin Jenkins (Graham Rowntree, 48 mins)
Keven Mealamu	2	Shane Byrne (Gordon Bulloch, 70 mins)
Greg Somerville	3	Julian White
Chris Jack (James Ryan, 77 mins)	4	Donncha O'Callaghan
Ali Williams	5	Paul O'Connell (Vice Captain)
Jerry Collins	6	Simon Easterby
Rodney So'oialo	7	Lewis Moody (Martyn Williams, 76 mins)
Sione Lauaki (Marty Holah, 40 mins)	8	Ryan Jones (Martin Corry, 68 mins)

Replacements (unused): Derren Whitcombe, Nick Evans, Doug Howlett

Tries: Smith, Williams, Umaga 2, Gear   **Try:** Moody

Cons: McAlister 5   **Con:** S Jones

Pen: McAlister   **Pens:** S Jones 4

Sin-bin: Umaga (8 mins), Collins (54 mins)

REFEREE: Jonathan Kaplan (South Africa)

Well played: The All Blacks parade the Series trophy, beautifully crafted by Waterford Crystal

The bare facts show that we have lost the Test Series, but I don't have to look too hard to find the positives out of our trip to New Zealand.

I see this Lions tour as a new start to my career, in the same way as the England tour to New Zealand and Australia kicked it off in 1998. Ironically, part two has started in similar way to part one, with defeat. But I have every confidence that 2005 will work in the same way as 1998 and make me a better player.

I will arrive back for the start of the season with a load of ideas about where to go next. Out in New Zealand I was learning not only on the field. I also took advantage of some time on my own to watch a lot of rugby league and union on the television.

The motivation to start my career again and go to another level is, I think, based on the fact that I am such a competitive person. It is a pride thing. Understanding I have an opportunity that I cannot afford to waste. I still have an overwhelming drive inside me to get better, to do special things in life.

That doesn't mean I'm not massively disappointed to be coming away from New Zealand without a Test series victory – I am. The Lions means an awful lot to me and after being on the wrong end of a 2-1 defeat previously, in Australia in 2001, I was determined to do all I could to change it this time.

To go out of the series midway through the Second Test is the biggest downside, along with the result, as it means my biggest regret was that I didn't get the chance to show exactly what I can do. But we can take a lot of pride from the way we responded to the defeat in the First Test.

You don't need any motivation for any match on a Lions tour, let alone a Test match. I hope everyone understands how proud everyone in the management and squad felt about playing for the Lions. They are very proud people in the way they have lived their lives to get here. They are people who won't accept second best and they believe that losing or not giving your best is simply unacceptable.

The First Test loss left everyone very down and most of the players I spoke to wanted to play the next day, so keen were they to put things right. In many ways we were

lucky to have a Second Test to go to. If this had been a World Cup we would have been out, so I expected the reaction we got in that Second Test.

We gave that match everything, but I was still left frustrated, as I don't think we showed everything we had. The lack of time to bring four nations together is tough. Some teams develop over years – as we saw with the England team that won the World Cup – so to do it in a matter of weeks was always going to be a difficult proposition.

In a romantic view the Brisbane First Test four years ago would happen all the time, but in the First Test this year it was the other end of spectrum, where things didn't function. Once in a while a match like that Brisbane Test comes round – when everything just clicks into place – and it shows you the potential of the Lions. They are hard days to achieve and even after them it is difficult to explain why they happened and so, therefore, it is difficult to replicate them.

The disappointing performances on this trip certainly haven't come from a lack of desire. The relationship between the Lions players was as good as it possibly could have been, but when you play a side like New Zealand you have to start strong. In the First Test we didn't. In the Second we did, but then we didn't hold on for long enough, letting New Zealand back in the game straight away and making life very difficult.

New Zealand is an incredible place to come and play rugby. Everyone seems to be involved in the game, or knows the game, which makes any rugby tour to New Zealand intense and very unforgiving.

On this tour I have learnt to enjoy my rugby more. I said I would do that at the start of the season, but it was just words then. I didn't quite know how to do that. Being here with the Welsh, the Irish and the Scots, I have learnt to enjoy the game more. On this tour I have learnt to embrace the occasion and I hope there will be many more occasions to come.

You Were Fan-tastic

"*Our fans have been fantastic. I went out and met some of them after that First Test and I had to buy them the drinks, rather than the other way around. I just wanted them to know how much we appreciated their support and how bad we felt for not performing to our real potential. This tour has given me the chance to enjoy this country and to meet players and fans who all share my love of the game.*" **Josh Lewsey**

"We had incredible support on the trip and although none of my immediate family were in New Zealand, there were people from my village of Glanaman who I knew. It gave us a huge lift. It was unbelievable and I certainly haven't experienced anything like it before. It's such a shame we couldn't win the series and give a little bit back to those supporters. It shows how special the Lions are, and what a big place they have in the hearts of rugby supporters, that so many came around the world to follow us. It's massive and I can't get over the support we've had."

Shane Williams

"The Lions fans were sensational – it is as simple as that. To see hundreds in the lobby of our hotel before I made my Test debut gave me and the rest of the boys such a lift, and then when we went outside there were hundreds more to give us a big send off. I remember in the team meeting, when we were waiting to have our jerseys presented, we could hear 'Bread of Heaven' being sung – full volume – in the hotel bar. Every one of the lads is so appreciative of the efforts they have made, and all we wish is that we could have delivered a series win for them!"
Lewis Moody

"One of the reasons why the midweek side was so successful was the fans. As a squad we realised that many supporters only came out for the last two weeks, so it was up to us to perform, particularly towards the end when the Test matches had started. The supporters were extraordinary. We managed to give them the chance to get behind the midweek side with the performances we put in, and by the end of the tour I think they had a bit of affection for us. Their loyalty was unstinting and we can only thank them for that. We won't remember this trip for results on the field, but we will remember it for the fans, especially the way they traveled to places like Dunedin and Invercargill in their thousands. There was a great atmosphere that went along with the Lions and that was something we will remember." **Gordon Bulloch**

"The fans have given us a massive lift on this trip. Their unbreakable spirit has been something to behold and the way they followed their team around the world – without a hint of any trouble – is a massive credit to them. We are very proud as a team of the fans who have travelled and we are grateful for the sacrifices they have made to be with us. To have so many people in one place, but to do everything respectfully and with passion, is incredible. They have offered us unconditional support on this trip and even when we have lost they haven't questioned us. You can't ask for any more than that. You want to repay that as much as you can and I believe the way for me to repay that is to practise my kicking, rest in my room and be the best player I can. I wanted to put in a performance that was acceptable to them, taking into account the money they've spent, the miles they have travelled and the sacrifices they have made." **Jonny Wilkinson**

The Lions lost the Series and to all those involved in the tour that is a huge disappointment. But I will still look back with a lot of pride on the trip. On the day we lost to the better side.

Rugby Union is one of the greatest team games and playing for or against the Lions is seen as one of the ultimate goals to achieve as a rugby player. The degree to which we have seen professionalism grow over the years, and the results of this professional approach, are seen in the current New Zealand team. The All Blacks have grown together and their coaches have been together a long time. That not only makes the rugby in New Zealand hugely challenging, but also makes it a fantastic place to tour whether as coach, player or supporter.

A key part of what I set out to achieve over the past year was to give the players the best chance of beating the All Blacks, given the challenge of marrying the tradition and history of the Lions with the professionalism of the modern rugby era. That meant providing the support network, the back up and the coaches to help performance on the field, all within the short time span that was the 2005 Lions. Everything was planned down to the finest detail - from the way that we handled the jetlag, through all the logistical arrangements for the two coaching set-ups, to having a dedicated coaching focus for each game.

Maybe if I could have my time again, if I could change one thing, it would have been better to say earlier on in the tour that "This is the Test team". There would obviously have been changes over the weeks, but to have been up front early on might have been better. It is easy to talk with hindsight, but I did what I thought was best, which was to give every player a chance to impress and play for selection. The 2005 Lions will always be judged on the Test results. However, as with every Lions Tour, we have seen players put in truly world-class performances in tough circumstances. Ryan Jones, Lewis Moody, Simon Easterby, Donncha O'Callaghan and Dwayne Peel, to name a few, showed what they were made of during the six challenging weeks.

There have been a number of Lions tours that have been unhappy trips, but I have really enjoyed this one. I know that this is the same for the players, the coaches and the support staff. I also think that every person on this tour has learnt something to take back to their home union and it presents an exciting and challenging time for rugby union going forward, with the New Zealand autumn 'Grand Slam' tour and the 2007 World Cup just around the corner.

The 2005 Lions had no past and has no future. You just have that period of six weeks to bring together the group of players, with all the history and ethos that makes a Lions Tour quite a romantic notion. But I am not a romantic coach. I work on real structure and process and that is probably why I found selection very difficult this time round. I was very conscious that I wanted this trip to be a happy, enjoyable one. I resolutely buy into the Lions ethos and history, but I see now that maybe the 2005 Lions needed a week longer together, and that the coaches needed more time to get to know the players. We certainly saw the characters from the four countries. Brian O'Driscoll gave immense leadership, whilst Gareth Thomas was superb on this trip. I had no idea what an inspirational person he is.

Despite losing the series, I said in a meeting before the final Test that there is not one person that I would have changed coming on this trip. Every one of the players gave their all on the pitch and for that I am hugely proud. I will always remember this Lions tour as a wonderful experience with a truly great bunch of players, coaches and staff.

Sir Clive Woodward

The 2005 British & Irish Lions Touring Party

Sir Clive Woodward (Head Coach), Bill Beaumont (Tour Manager), John Feehan (Chief Executive), Louise Ramsay (Team Manager), Andy Robinson (Coach), Eddie O'Sullivan (Coach), Phil Larder (Coach), Ian McGeechan (Coach), Gareth Jenkins (Coach), Mike Ford (Coach), Dave Alred (Coach), David McHugh (Specialist Advisor), Dave Reddin (Fitness Coach), Craig White (Fitness Coach), Dr James Robson (Head Doctor), Dr Gary O'Driscoll (Doctor), Phil Pask (Physiotherapist), Stuart Barton (Physiotherapist), Bob Stewart (Physiotherapist), Richard Wegrzyk (Masseur), Tony Biscombe (Video Analysis), Gavin Scott (Video Analysis), Alastair Campbell (Media Advisor), Louisa Cheetham (Media Manager), Marcus Jansa (Media Assistant), Ben Wilson (Media Assistant), Dave Tennison (Kit Technician), Dave Pearson (Kit Assistant), Dave Campbell (Chef), Richard Smith (Legal Support)

THE PLAYERS

Neil Back (England), Iain Balshaw (England), Gordon Bulloch (Scotland), Shane Byrne (Ireland), Brent Cockbain (Wales), Gareth Cooper (Wales), Martin Corry (England), Mark Cueto (England), Chris Cuisiter (Scotland), Lawrence Dallaglio (England), Gordon D'Arcy (Ireland), Matt Dawson (England), Simon Easterby (Ireland), Will Greenwood (England), Danny Grewcock (England), John Hayes (Ireland), Gavin Henson (Wales),

Denis Hickie (Ireland), Richard Hill (England), Charlie Hodgson (England), Shane Horgan (Ireland), Gethin Jenkins (Wales), Ryan Jones (Wales), Stephen Jones (Wales), Ben Kay (England), Josh Lewsey (England), Lewis Moody (England), Geordan Murphy (Ireland), Donncha O'Callaghan (Ireland), Paul O'Connell (Ireland), Brian O'Driscoll, (Captain) (Ireland), Ronan O'Gara (Ireland), Malcolm O'Kelly (Ireland), Michael Owen (Wales), Dwayne Peel (Wales), Jason Robinson (England), Graham Rowntree (England), Tom Shanklin (Wales), Simon Shaw (England), Andy Sheridan (England), Ollie Smith (England), Matt Stevens (England), Simon Taylor (Scotland), Gareth Thomas (Wales), Steve Thompson (England), Andy Titterrell (England), Jason White (Scotland), Julian White (England), Jonny Wilkinson (England), Martyn Williams (Wales), Shane Williams (Wales)

Notes on players:

Iain Balshaw pulled out of the Lions squad due to injury prior to the team's departure to New Zealand and was replaced by Mark Cueto.

Lawrence Dallaglio, Richard Hill, Brian O'Driscoll, Malcolm O'Kelly, Tom Shanklin and Simon Taylor's tours were cut short due to injury.

Replacement players called out to join the tour in New Zealand were Brent Cockbain, Simon Easterby, Ryan Jones, Simon Shaw and Jason White.

THE SQUAD	Pos	Born	Age	Club	2005 Lions Tour All Games App	Try	Pts	Tests App	Try	Pts	Lions Career All Games App	Try	Pts	Tests App	Try	Pts	Test Career International Caps Nat	Caps	Try	Pts
Neil Back	FL	16 Jan 69	36	Leicester T.	2+1	1	5	1	-	-	14+2	5	25	4+1	1	5	EN	63+3	16	83
Gordon Bulloch	H	26 Mar 75	30	Glasgow	4+2	-	-	0+1	-	-	5+5	-	-	0+2	-	-	SC	71+4	4	20
Shane Byrne	H	18 Jul 71	33	Leinster	4+3	-	-	2+1	-	-	4+3	-	-	2+1	-	-	IR	28+10	3	15
Brent Cockbain	L	15 Nov 74	30	Ospreys	0+2	-	-	-	-	-	0+2	-	-	-	-	-	WA	19+1	-	-
Gareth Cooper	SH	7 Jul 79	26	Dragons	2+2	1	5	-	-	-	2+2	1	5	-	-	-	WA	19+7	6	30
Martin Corry	BR	12 Oct 73	31	Leicester T.	5+4	2	10	1+2	-	-	11+5	2	10	3+3	-	-	EN	18+19	3	15
Mark Cueto	W	26 Dec 79	25	Sale Sharks	4+1	3	15	-	-	-	4+1	3	15	1	-	-	EN	8	8	40
Chris Cusiter	SH	13 Jun 82	23	Borders	3+2	-	-	-	-	-	3+2	-	-	-	-	-	SC	16	1	5
Lawrence Dallaglio	BR	10 Aug 72	32	Wasps	1	-	-	-	-	-	10	1	5	3	-	-	EN	68+5	15	75
Gordon D'Arcy	C	10 Feb 80	25	Leinster	5+2	2	10	-	-	-	5+2	2	10	-	-	-	IR	7+5	2	10
Matt Dawson	SH	31 Oct 72	32	Wasps	2+4	-	-	0+2	-	-	10+9	3	36	4+3	2	10	EN	52+18	15	96
Simon Easterby	FL	21 Jul 75	29	Llanelli Scarlets	4+1	1	5	2	1	5	4+1	1	5	2	1	5	IR	38+4	4	20
Will Greenwood	C	20 Oct 72	32	Harlequins	4+1	1	5	1+1	-	-	13+2	3	15	1+1	-	-	EN	50+5	31	155
Danny Grewcock	L	7 Nov 72	32	Bath	3+2	-	-	0+1	-	-	9+2	1	5	3+1	-	-	EN	40+17	2	10
John Hayes	P	2 Nov 73	31	Munster	5	-	-	-	-	-	5	-	-	-	-	-	IR	53+1	2	10
Gavin Henson	C	1 Feb 82	23	Ospreys	4	2	10	1	-	-	4	2	10	1	-	-	WA	14+2	3	124
Denis Hickie	W	13 Feb 76	29	Leinster	5	-	-	-	-	-	5	-	-	-	-	-	IR	51	25	125
Richard Hill	BR	23 May 73	32	Saracens	3	-	-	1	-	-	12+1	1	5	5	-	-	EN	68+3	12	60
Charlie Hodgson	FH	12 Nov 80	24	Sale Sharks	4	1	53	-	-	-	4	1	53	-	-	-	EN	15+4	4	154
Shane Horgan	C	18 Jul 78	26	Leinster	1+6	1	5	0+3	-	-	1+6	1	5	0+3	-	-	IR	36+1	12	60
Gethin Jenkins	P	17 Nov 80	24	Cardiff Blues	5+2	1	5	3	-	-	5+2	1	5	3	-	-	WA	20+11	3	15
Ryan Jones	No 8	13 Mar 81	24	Ospreys	3+1	1	5	2+1	-	-	3+1	1	5	2+1	-	-	WA	7+1	1	5
Stephen Jones	FH	8 Dec 77	27	Clermont(FR)	3+1	-	22	2+1	-	14	3+1	-	22	2+1	-	14	WA	41+7	5	441
Ben Kay	L	14 Dec 75	29	Leicester T.	4+1	-	-	1	-	-	4+1	-	-	1	-	-	EN	36+4	2	10
Josh Lewsey	W	30 Nov 76	28	Wasps	6	2	10	3	-	-	6	2	10	3	-	-	EN	33+1	21	105
Lewis Moody	BR	12 Jun 78	27	Leicester T.	5	1	5	2	1	5	5	1	5	2	1	5	EN	23+8	8	40
Geordan Murphy	FB	19 Apr 78	27	Leicester T.	7	3	15	1	-	-	7	3	15	1	-	-	IR	28+3	15	80
Donncha O'Callaghan	L	23 Mar 79	26	Munster	7	-	-	2	-	-	7	-	-	2	-	-	IR	3+13	-	-
Paul O'Connell	L	20 Oct 79	25	Munster	5	-	-	3	-	-	5	-	-	3	-	-	IR	25+4	4	20
Brian O'Driscoll	C	21 Jan 79	26	Leinster	4	1	5	1	-	-	10	5	25	4	1	5	IR	58+1	27	147
Ronan O'Gara	FH	7 Mar 77	28	Munster	2+5	2	49	0+1	-	-	4+7	2	75	0+1	-	-	IR	38+14	7	525
Michael Owen	BR	7 Nov 80	24	Dragons	6+1	-	-	-	-	-	6+1	-	-	-	-	-	WA	20+4	1	5
Dwayne Peel	SH	31 Aug 81	23	Llanelli Scarlets	5	1	5	3	-	-	5	1	5	3	-	-	WA	22+19	4	20
Jason Robinson	W	30 Jul 74	30	Sale Sharks	4	1	5	2	-	-	10+1	11	55	5	2	10	EN	35+4	22	110
Graham Rowntree	P	18 Apr 71	34	Leicester T.	4+2	-	-	0+2	-	-	9+3	1	5	0+2	-	-	EN	45+7	-	-
Tom Shanklin	C	24 Nov 79	25	Cardiff Blues	2+1	1	5	-	-	-	2+1	1	5	-	-	-	WA	25+8	15	75
Simon Shaw	L	1 Sep 73	31	Wasps	5	-	-	-	-	-	11+1	2	10	-	-	-	EN	19+9	2	10
Andrew Sheridan	P	1 Nov 79	25	Sale Sharks	2+3	-	-	-	-	-	2+3	-	-	-	-	-	EN	0+1	-	-
Ollie Smith	C	14 Aug 82	22	Leicester T.	4+1	2	10	-	-	-	4+1	2	10	-	-	-	EN	1+4	-	-
Matt Stevens	P	1 Oct 82	22	Bath	3+2	-	-	-	-	-	3+2	-	-	-	-	-	EN	3+2	-	-
Gareth Thomas	FB	25 Jul 74	30	Toulouse(FR)	4	2	10	3	1	5	4	2	10	3	1	5	WA	79+4	34	170
Steve Thompson	H	15 Jul 78	26	Northampton	2+4	-	-	1+1	-	-	2+4	-	-	1+1	-	-	EN	36+3	40	15
Andy Titterrell	H	10 Jan 81	24	Sale Sharks	2+1	-	-	-	-	-	2+1	-	-	-	-	-	EN	0+4	-	-
Jason White	L	17 Apr 78	27	Sale Sharks	1	-	-	-	-	-	1	-	-	-	-	-	SC	36+10	4	20
Julian White	BR	14 May 73	32	Leicester T.	5+1	-	-	3	-	-	5+1	-	-	3	-	-	EN	24+4	-	-
Jonny Wilkinson	FH	25 May 79	26	Newcastle F.	4	-	44	2	-	11	9	2	116	5	1	47	EN	25+2	2	407
Martyn Williams	BR	1 Sep 75	29	Cardiff Blues	6+1	1	5	0+1	-	-	10+1	1	5	0+1	-	-	WA	44+9	7	38
Shane Williams	W	26 Feb 77	28	Ospreys	5	6	30	1	-	-	5	6	30	1	-	-	WA	27+2	24	120
Penalty Tries					-			-												

Key: 4+1 in App column denotes 4 starts plus one game as a sub.

		App	Try	Pts	App	Try	Pts		
LIONS TOTALS FOR		180+60	40	353	45+18	3	40	All games: Pld 12, Won 7, Drawn 1, Lost 4	
TOTALS AGAINST			21	245		12	107	Test matches: Pld 3, Won 0, Lost 3	

THE KICKERS	2005 Lions Tour All Games Miss	Success%	C	PG	DG	Tests C	PG	DG	Lions Career All Games C	PG	DG	Tests C	PG	DG	Kicking Success Good	Att	Career%
Matt Dawson	-	-	-	-	-	-	-	-	6	3	-	-	-	-	9	14	64.29%
Charlie Hodgson	5	80.00%	12	8	-	-	-	-	12	8	-	-	-	-	20	25	80.00%
Stephen Jones	3	72.73%	2	6	-	1	4	-	2	6	-	1	4	-	8	11	72.73%
Ronan O'Gara	9	64.00%	9	7	-	-	-	-	22	7	-	-	-	-	29	43	67.44%
Jonny Wilkinson	4	80.00%	4	12	-	1	3	-	17	24	-	6	10	-	41	55	74.55%
LIONS TOTALS	21	72.73%	26	30	-	1	4	-									
OPPONENTS	9	85.48%	19	34	-	10	9	-									

Stats provided by Stuart Farmer Media Services

Vision Sports Publishing

2 Coombe Gardens,

London, SW20 0QU

www.visionsp.co.uk

This First Edition Published by

Vision Sports Publishing in 2005

Pictures © Getty Images, British Lions Ltd, and Vision Sports Publishing

Text © Vision Sports Publishing and British Lions Ltd

Printed and bound in Italy by

Printer Trento Srl

Paper is 130gsm Gardamatt Art

A CIP catalogue record for this book is available from the British Library

ISBN 1-9053260-4-1

THE TOUGHEST TEST

Editor: Jim Drewett

Words: Paul Morgan

Design: Neal Cobourne (rkidesign@btinternet.com)

Production: Ulrika Ahlander

PHOTOGRAPHY BY GETTY IMAGES

Getty Images photographers Dave Rogers and Sean Botterill spent six weeks on the road in
New Zealand photographing the Lions tour. A legend in the world of rugby photography,
Dave Rogers has covered more than 300 rugby union internationals and 2005 was his
seventh Lions tour. Sean Botterill has covered football, cricket and rugby World Cups and four
Olympic Games but says the Lions tour to New Zealand was "the one major event I wanted
to see and photograph".

Additional photography. AFP/Getty Images

Additional 'fans' photography. Toby Trotman

Behind-the-scenes photography. Gavin Scott

ACKNOWLEDGEMENTS

Vision Sports Publishing would like to thank the British & Irish Lions for giving us the privilege
of producing the official book of the 2005 Tour to New Zealand. Thanks to all the players for
taking time out to give their input, to Sir Clive Woodward and Bill Beaumont for their
thoughtful contributions, to Dave Kavanagh for his enthusiasm for the project, to Louisa
Cheetham for all her assistance from start to finish and to Gavin Scott for allowing us to use
his brilliant behind-the-scenes pictures. Thanks also to Mark Spoors of Big Red Management
for bringing VSP and the Lions together, to Rick Mayston, Mark Webbon, Neil Loft and Justin
Davies at Getty Images and to Karen Hughes and Tim Harte and everyone at Printer Trento.
A special acknowledgement must also go to the hard-working editorial team - Paul Morgan of
Rugby World magazine and Neal Cobourne for his superb design work, and to Stuart Farmer
Media Services and the NZRU and all the provincial teams for their assistance with the stats.
Though working on this project has left us all with a feeling of "what might have been", we are
proud to have played some part in this historic Lions tour.